EVERYONE'S A

GENIUS

Lance—
Keep living out your
leadership genius!

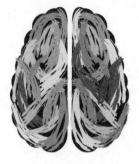

EVERYONE'S A
GENIUS

UNLEASHING CREATIVITY

FOR THE SAKE OF THE WORLD

ALAN BRIGGS

THOMAS NELSON

Since 1798

Published in Nashville, Tennessee, by Thomas Nelson. Thomas Nelson is a registered trademark of HarperCollins Christian Publishing, Inc.

Thomas Nelson titles may be purchased in bulk for educational, business, fund-raising, or sales promotional use. For information, please e-mail SpecialMarkets@ThomasNelson.com.

Unless otherwise indicated, all Scripture quotations are taken from the ESV˙ Bible (the Holy Bible, English Standard Version˙), copyright © 2001 by Crossway, a publishing ministry of Good News Publishers. Used by permission. All rights reserved.

Scripture quotations marked THE MESSAGE are taken from *The Message*. Copyright © by Eugene H. Peterson 1993, 1994, 1995, 1996, 2000, 2001, 2002. Used by permission of NavPress. All rights reserved. Represented by Tyndale House Publishers, Inc.

Italics in Scripture quotations reflect the author's added emphasis.

Any Internet addresses, phone numbers, or company or product information printed in this book are offered as a resource and are not intended in any way to be or to imply an endorsement by Thomas Nelson, nor does Thomas Nelson vouch for the existence, content, or services of these sites, phone numbers, companies, or products beyond the life of this book.

ISBN 978-0-7180-8229-1 (eBook)
ISBN 978-0-7180-4253-0 (TP)

Library of Congress Control Number: 2017944690

Printed in the United States of America
17 18 19 20 21   LSC   10 9 8 7 6 5 4 3 2 1

For Betti, Manny, Eli, and Mercy
You are geniuses.
You're going to change the world, and
you're changing us in the process.

About Leadership✻Network

Leadership Network fosters innovation movements that activate the church to greater impact. We help shape the conversations and practices of pacesetter churches in North America and around the world. The Leadership Network mind-set identifies church leaders with forward-thinking ideas—and helps them to catalyze those ideas resulting in movements that shape the church.

Together with HarperCollins Christian Publishing, the biggest name in Christian books, the NEXT imprint of Leadership Network moves ideas to implementation for leaders to take their ideas to form, substance, and reality. Placed in the hands of other church leaders, that reality begins spreading from one leader to the next . . . and to the next . . . and to the next, where that idea begins to flourish into a full-grown movement that creates a real, tangible impact in the world around it.

NEXT: A Leadership Network Resource
committed to helping you grow your next idea.

leadnet.org/NEXT

CONTENTS

CONTENTS

FOREWORD

You are holding an important, timely book. Alan takes us on a journey that explores both our greatest opportunity as leaders and the church's greatest opportunity in our lifetime.

First, Alan will ignite your imagination and challenge you to embrace your most creative self. It has been said that you can only give as much as you know about yourself to as much as you know about God. Too many leaders today are living with their God-given talent still half buried, thus underappreciated and underutilized. Are you a believer in your own God-given genius? Have you unearthed the treasure that is God's divine design of your Ephesians 2:10 personal calling? Have you really tended to your life dreams? With every turn of the page, Alan's biblical and practical vision will draw out your calling and encourage you to cocreate a more beautiful and powerful life. Allow this book to become a place of self-discovery: a place to be stirred and stretched and set free to become more like the real you. That's always your greatest opportunity as a leader.

Second, and even more importantly, Alan hits the bulls-eye on what I believe to be an unprecedented opportunity for the church—seeing your church as a genius factory of limitless redemptive potential. Our standard drive-through seminars to get people plugged into volunteer roles in today's church are hopelessly limited. After decades of "find your ministry" programming, I wholeheartedly agree with Alan that we still have a screaming need: "Most people sitting in the pews don't sense they are a part of God's great mission to redeem all things."

Alan is as much of a pioneer in showing us this opportunity as he is in guiding our next steps. Chapter by chapter, you will find new perspective, language, and tools to engage your flock toward the highest and best use of their lives. Several chapters leaped out of the book with groundbreaking insights; each one is worth more than the price of the book. And best of all, the principles are relevant for every faith tribe as well as every church size. Whether you are a missional thinker, tinkerer, or practitioner, this book won't disappoint.

May we all deploy the genius within us and around us for God's glory.

Will Mancini,
cofounder of Life Younique
and author of *God Dreams*

INTRODUCTION

AWAKE, O GENIUS

There is a space in our lives, a zone of competency, where we are on fire, fully alive, and thriving. Often when you're doing this time flies. You're not exerting yourself, but somehow you are making an impact. I played baseball for years. The ball hits the bat on this one-inch section at just the right millisecond and explodes into the centerfield bleachers. The farthest home runs I ever hit felt effortless. The same is true of leadership: some of the most impacting things you'll ever do seem most natural.

Most of us have been taught to muscle up and swing hard with everything we've got. Muster up focused effort, and put your whole life into something. Hit the ball as far as you can. Crush it! But those swings usually result in strikeouts. The training has been done. You've learned your swing. You've practiced it thousands of times. All you need to do is swing your bat. Our culture seems to whisper "grip it and rip it" when all you need to do is know your swing and try to make contact. You'll know when it hits the sweet spot.

We are not limited by our genius; we are guided by it. God didn't create you as 10 percent complete just for you to realize you lack the other 90 percent of how others excel. Yet we spend much of our lives focusing on our weaknesses, the few things we can't do well. God created you uniquely as *you*. There is no test or exam to be God's kid. God doesn't see two groups: His gifted children and the rest of us. God did not give the Great Commission to the extremely gifted, the church staff, and the public speaker; He gave it to all of us.

Why Is This Book Crucial Right Now?

This message is crucial right now. We must recover a proper theology of creativity. I see three things permeating our culture right now. Fear, self-obsession, and longings for the good life.

Fear

Declining numbers in our churches in an increasingly post-Christian culture breeds desperation that can take us to extreme fear. Many church budgets are shrinking and leaving pastors wondering if they will continue to receive a full salary from their church. Strictly based on making a living, being a pastor is not exactly the best ROI on your education today. We need to see the gospel potential in some of these cultural shifts, namely, the great potential for nonpaid leaders in the church, who bear no ministerial title, to be unleashed in unique ways.

Self-obsession

We live in a selfie culture that's fixated on being famous, known, followed, successful, hip, and envied. A friend works as a guidance counselor for one of the fastest-growing Christian universities in the country. The number-one thing incoming freshmen want to be in their lives: *famous*. Dear Lord, help us. Ultimately this is a misplaced desire to apply our genius to real-world issues, but this culture of self is spinning out of control. Before we get too worked up, remember that at least we aren't gathering in arenas to watch wild animals rip Christians apart as they did in ancient Rome. Things can always get worse.

Longings for the Good Life

People are asking a lot of questions about the good life (you can read extensively about this topic in James K. A. Smith's *You Are What You Love*). Millennials are highlighting longings for a different way of life that has great potential to influence our culture in robust ways through work, neighboring, craft, generosity, and relationships. There is great potential here in a hungry and longing world.

———

Continuing to read the words on these pages is a risk. It might change your view of everyone you are preaching to and the teams you are leading. This might resonate with a mind shift from church-centric to kingdom-centric. This might help you see your city differently. You might find a gift economy within your church that leads you to send leaders whom you have previously tried your best to retain. These words might also unlock something within you that you never knew could matter to God. Perhaps God will use this book to take you on a journey toward a more appropriate theology of creativity. Yes, it's a risk, but a risk we simply must take. I dare you.

CHAPTER 1

WHERE DOES GENIUS COME FROM?

When one is loved, she can create better.
—Ana Ros

When your entire vocation is viewed as mission,
there are very few hours that aren't discipleship.
—Preston Sprinkle

There is not a square inch in the whole domain
of our human existence over which Christ, who
is Sovereign over all, does not cry, Mine!
—Abraham Kuyper

Where Does Your Creativity Come From?

Painters flee to the edge of the pines with canvas and brushes in hand. Writers tap into inspiration in their favorite coffee shop. Musicians find a quiet space to riff on the melodies flowing through their heads. There are no rules for when or where. All honest artists have to address the origins of their creativity.

Culture is shifting in massive ways right now. One exciting shift I see is a move toward celebrating and affirming different gifts and special abilities. Companies and churches are hiring differently. Creative types and out-of-the-box thinkers are being celebrated. There is more space in our culture for people who primarily live in the right side of their brains. Our culture is celebrating creativity. However, it seems we are a bit behind the curve on this idea of genius in the church. Perhaps it feels too prideful to talk about, or maybe it's hard for us to learn to celebrate gifts outside the spiritual gifts lists we find in Scripture.

One of the most electric modern celebrations of creativity happens at TED events (TED stands for technology, education, and design). These environments are infectious (and a tad pretentious) gatherings of innovators, creatives, and world changers. TED talks have become the secular sermons of our day. Leaders celebrate and even worship the genius of the leaders on stage at these TED events. I often pick out talks to watch and discuss with my kids.

Of all the TED talks I've watched only one has arrested me. It was by author Elizabeth Gilbert. Her talk grabbed my attention because of her humility and desire to tackle a question we are all asking: Where does creativity come from? After becoming a bestselling author through her wildly popular book *Eat, Pray, Love,* she hit a crisis moment. *Were her best days behind her? Could she ever produce something this successful again?* She began searching for the elusive creative genius. She headed back in time for a view of genius that made more sense than it does in our society today.

The ancient Greeks referred to the spirit of creativity as a *daemon*, and the ancient Romans personified creativity this way: "a genius was a guardian spirit, a god who accompanied people throughout life, connecting them to the divine."[1] It was a disembodied spirit or muse that visited artists and other creatives. Thus ancient peoples might say, "You *have* a genius," rather than our vernacular "You *are* a genius."

Greek and Roman societies did not believe humans were the locus of creativity, but rather creativity came from somewhere and something else. What people created was more about something that happened to them and less about something they possessed or expressed. Darrin M. McMahon observed, "The Roman genius, without question, was very far from the modern 'genius.'"[2]

During the Renaissance, this perspective on creativity changed. The emerging philosophy of humanism shifted the focus to the creative as a genius. Humanity was celebrated rather than invisible spirits. Artists, sculptors, painters, and composers were now geniuses. Today, we might call a jack of all trades a Renaissance man.

In fact, today's prevailing definition of *genius* is relatively new. "The term *genius*, as it is currently defined, goes back to the tail end of the eighteenth century."[3]

So we have to ask, which view is closer to reality: antiquity, early humanism, or our modern world?

The ancient view of genius sounds more like God-inspired, God-breathed creativity than what our culture believes today. The ancients were puzzled as to how frail humans could create things so inspiring, and so they perceived a spirit of genius behind it all. Someone else, they believed, must drive humans and shape their work. When we *have* a genius, we are stewards, co-creators. During the Renaissance, humans took credit for their achievements. This was a grave mistake, and we are still suffering from it today.

When we *are* the genius behind the creative process, the pressure falls on our frail shoulders. Writers hit blocks. Painters hit dry spells. Speakers fumble over their words. We all have moments when we feel creative and others when we can't produce a thing.

The deification of *genius* has led us into some faulty thinking. We begin to believe certain people are born as superheroes and brainiacs who fly at a much higher level than the rest of us, and some even see them as worthy of our worship. Perhaps this is why so many celebrities break down and crash and burn these days. We've wrongly believed the myth that our world has a few wildly creative people while we're stuck in the group simply labeled "the rest of us."

I am here to tell you, contrary to popular belief, *everyone* has access to the spirit of creativity. Every human is formed in the image of God, the *imago dei*.

The good news is this: everyone is a genius.

The bad news is this: we aren't exactly the genius, but God is the genius behind us all.

The real news is this: we are not the genius, but we *have* a genius.

You might read this and say, "I'm no genius." Perhaps you wrestle with continual noncreativity. You don't write songs. You don't solve complex math equations. You don't write screen plays or pitch million-dollar ideas. You've already counted yourself out of the creative conversation.

If that's the case, then this book is for you. Don't put it down just yet. Whether you believe me or not, *you are a creative being.* You were crafted in the image of the Creator. You are a genius because you *have* a genius. We were fashioned in the mind and in the image of a creative God.

Some of you regularly wrestle with your creativity. Perhaps you write songs, labor on paintings, chase the illusive perfect photo, experiment with different mediums, design your own clothes, play with lyrics, and twist rhymes. You struggle to know how this fits with others and how to express something that feels so innately *you.* You wonder how you can use your God-given creativity for God-centered purposes. Chances are you have been misunderstood along the way. Some people have affirmed your gifts and talents, but most have been confused by them. This book is for you.

Perhaps you are like me, and you fall somewhere in between. I have often compared myself to others and concluded I am not a creative and will never be graced with the kind of creativity others have. I have also had many days when I had no idea how to fully express my creativity around others. Songs that made sense in my head didn't resonate with others, and phrases that made sense to me only confused those who heard them when I said them out loud.

But I am also a pastor. I help to guide a dynamic congregation whom the living God is constantly shaping. I seek to affirm and recognize the creativity and the genius God has placed in those around me. I spend a lot of time equipping leaders and church planters for how they can freely live in the image of the Creator for the sake of the world. And that's the real focus of this book: to recognize everyone's genius and help geniuses apply their creativity for the sake of the world. The witness of the church is at stake.

Framing Genius

Let's take a minute to frame the conversation of genius and why it matters to God's kingdom.

Your genius is *given by God, confirmed in community*, and aimed at *kingdom impact*. Don't worry, I will break down this statement as we proceed through the book.

The topic of creativity stirs up a lot of emotion. A few people get excited to talk about it, but most just shut it down as quickly as they can. And that's exactly why the conversation about genius is so crucial.

When I talk with others about creativity, I get a few standard reactions.

"I'm not creative at all." A friend has said this to me many times, but I see something different when I look at her life. She has always been able to re-create herself. Without much education, she has navigated the mortgage business, started several small businesses on the side, and learned to sustain life at a young age. Yet she defines creativity too narrowly. Folks look up to her, and she looks down on herself.

"No one understands my creativity." A friend grieves that her creativity was stifled when she was a child. Those around her pushed her aside, as if her creativity were a cute detail she would graduate from some day and move into the real world. She always felt undervalued, and to this day she struggles to know how to express her creativity and enjoy the mind God has given

her. She feels she needs to turn off the switch and simply be the person others want her to be.

"I wish I was creative." A friend looked up to visual artists, but he never saw himself in the role of a creative, because he never created visible works of art. He is very literal, very serious, and very calculated, and he thought that amounted to a lack of creativity. God rescued him from a life of addiction, and he has to be incredibly creative to figure out how to live a new narrative and follow God into marriage and fatherhood.

"I used to be creative." People remember a time when they created art. Today they've gotten busy with the perils of real life: bills, busyness, schedules, kids, and occasional boredom. A friend has taken his artistic creativity into the medical world, where he invests himself in the marvels of modern medicine. The human body became his canvas.

Untapped Potential

There is a massive untapped potential in our churches. While pastors and leadership teams often get the chance to attend conferences, work on their leadership craft, and analyze their gifts, most of the people in their congregations don't have the same opportunities. Most of the people sitting in the pews or comfy church chairs during weekend services don't sense they are part of God's great mission to redeem all things. Most unpaid church leaders don't believe they have anything to contribute to this needy world.

We have accidentally made our congregations passive. They've gotten the message they are not invited into ministry and they should get busy filling sanctuary seats, filling an offering plate, and filling the serving roles we are desperate to fill. But nothing could be further from the truth! Every person *is* a genius because we *have* a genius. Every person has been commissioned by Jesus Himself with the Great Commission. Every follower of Jesus is invited into ministry. Every person's gifts and talents can be unleashed in an outward direction for the sake of a needy world.

We need to rediscover a proper theology of creativity. Let's go back to the beginning. These are three significant soundbites from the creation narrative.

> "Let us make human beings in our image, make them reflecting our nature."
> —Genesis 1:26 THE MESSAGE

> God looked over everything he had made;
>   it was so good, so very good!
> —Genesis 1:31 THE MESSAGE

> When God created the human race, he made it godlike, with a nature akin to God.
> —Genesis 5:1 THE MESSAGE

We steward creativity; we don't actually create it. When we think *we* are the genius, it leads us into fear and anxiety, because it all depends on us. When we know God is the genius, the pressure is off of us because it's *His* message and we are *His* scribes. It's *His* poem, and we recite it. It's *His* song, and we are in the choir. It's *His* dance, and we are taking choreography cues. It's *His* novel, and we are simply holding the pen. It's *His* sermon, and we are just reciting it.

When we believe we are the source of creativity, we get all the credit and all the pressure. When we labor to generate creativity, we get stressed out. We will feel the depths of failure when we fall short.

When we believe God generates the creativity in us, this leads us instead to a posture of stewardship. When we realize creativity is inspired by God, He can get the worship. He can handle the pressure. Stewards take care of someone else's resources. Owners create and generate. Our theology of creativity is directly related to our theology of the Creator.

God, Bestselling Author of Creativity

Yes, we have a genius: the living God created us in His image. We are all co-creators, no matter how linear, left-brained, uncreative, or dull we might believe we are. There are extreme consequences for not recognizing creativity. If we believe we are not creative beings, we will avoid creating and simply copy others. Neither is healthy, and neither is inspiring. The best things we will ever create don't come from us but are on loan to us.[4]

I would have called myself an uncreative, but I had ideas, dreams, and ambitions, and I knew how to start things and lead people. I hadn't learned any particular craft or medium, so the creative visions in my head were never translated into something I was proud to show my friends. I would come home from fishing with beautiful pieces of driftwood, but I was never skilled enough to make them into something I was proud to show off. I tried a few times, and it just looked like mangled driftwood.

I have always loved shaping environments. My mom

reminded me a few years ago that I always loved to make my room look homey and inviting. Though this is hardly a talent, hardly creativity, her words stuck with me. Today our home is the center of our family canvas. Friends and neighbors gather there to find refuge from their sometimes brutal routines. Our walls are covered with reclaimed wood from pallets and fences I foraged. I poured concrete countertops with a friend. (I nearly broke my friend's leg when the first countertop snapped during transport, but we don't need to talk about that.)

My canvas is people. Much of the inspiration for my "people art" comes from my images of Jesus hanging out with notorious sinners at parties. Perhaps I am trying to re-create the scene from Matthew's house.

It took years to see this in myself. I used to think everyone found deep joy in having their friends and neighbors over, cooking for them or sharing some hot coffee on a cold morning. As we began to make neighboring a focus in our family, we bought the home we had been renting. Suddenly I could make all the changes I wanted to make to the space. People entered our home and commented on the environment. They felt welcomed, loved, and well-fed (the trifecta of hosting). It was as if they were curling up next to the fire of community to enjoy the warmth and the glow. As people started to echo this back to us, I began to see the power in it. Friends had to affirm that what we were doing mattered to them.

Sometimes I ask people to trace their income streams to their source and find God there. The same is true of creativity. Genius doesn't come from us, and it's not for us. God has created us to create, but He wants us to aim our creativity toward joining His mission and blessing His world.

The Leadership and Genius Debate

Debates continue today (and always will) around what leadership and genius truly are. *Is it nature or nurture? Did God give it, or did we learn it? Is it a gift or a skill?* The answer is yes! It is nature and nurture, God gives it, and we learn it. It's a gift and a skill. It can be effortless, and we need to work hard at it. I have watched abilities squandered by incredibly talented people who were too proud or too lazy to work hard. I have watched proverbial tortoises beat the hares through hard work and humility. It takes work and sacrifice to live into the things God has for us. A gift doesn't negate hard work. When we are given a gift, we have to work hard to hone it.

In short, leadership takes work. Max De Pree noted, "Leadership is an art, something to be learned over time. . . . Leadership is more tribal than scientific, more a weaving of relationships than an amassing of information."[5] Time, hard work, and the voices of others will help you grow into the kind of leader God has created you to be. This "weaving of relationships" De Pree talks about is crucial. Others remind us of our gifting and our areas of struggle. The most effective leaders and creatives develop over time with the humility to see we are merely stewards of our lives.

Blessed to Be a Blessing

Our call to live as blessers for the sake of the world began in the book of Genesis:

> Now the LORD said to Abram, "Go from your country and your kindred and your father's house to the land that I will

show you. And I will make of you a great nation, and I will bless you and make your name great, so that you will be a blessing. I will bless those who bless you, and him who dishonors you I will curse, and in you all the families of the earth shall be blessed." (12:1–3)

This great exchange between God and Abraham starts with a command to go. This journey of faith for his family would not be a small one, but they were to leave comfort and normalcy behind and go. There's not a whole lot of security in the destination of "the land that I will show you," especially when you are leaving your country, your family, and your father's house.

The next statement is a promise from God: *I will bless you and make your name great.* Abraham will not be able to take credit for the legacy he will leave as a forefather and blesser. Here's the catch: God will make Abraham's name great *so* he will be a blesser to others. The blessing of God isn't just for us—it's a gift to be shared.

As people who have been blessed beyond belief by the Creator, we are to go and spread blessing. The work of our hands is, perhaps, the most practical way we can redirect the blessing of God to others. In using the creative juices God has given us, we become a foretaste of the kingdom of God. People get glimpses of beauty so divine they are perplexed as to where it came from. Genius is not *from* us, and it's not just *for* us.

Great artists understand their art isn't just for them. Beauty and creativity should be shared. Love should be shared. Gifts should be shared. Our talents should be shared with a world longing to see the good gifts of the Creator, but a world looking for them in all the wrong places. We are servants who come on behalf of the King. Millard Fuller, founder of Habitat for Humanity, said, "I see life as both a gift and a responsibility. My responsibility is to use what God has given me to help his people in need." He had a proper view of servant leadership that has led to multitudes of families having roofs over their heads. Proverbs 16:3 reminds us, "Commit your work to the LORD, and your plans will be established.". We take this verse out of context a lot; it's not about our success but about God's success.

Far too often we look to the powers of our day to put a price tag on us and tell us our worth. This always leaves us feeling used up, squandered, and hoodwinked. People look to the government, to social media, and to the things they can compile to tell them their worth.[6] We need to leave these value-seeking narratives behind and embrace the narrative of the servant leader. We are stewards who serve our King, His kingdom, and people He dearly loves.

When we fall in love with other narratives, we will start to play by their rules. If we get stuck in the world of media and television, we will be looking for fifteen minutes of fame.[7] Where has mundane faith gone in our world of fame, fortune, and recognition? We are part of an alternative community, a family of faith. In their prophetic book *People of the Truth*, Robert E. Webber and Rodney Clapp called this "a community of giftedness." They wrote,

> Through the cross the church learns that life is a gift and that to live is to give . . . The community of giftedness is composed of persons who have learned they do not own themselves. Their lives are not self-controlled and self-managed, but given up to their Giver. The church is a community of people happy to confess, 'We do not belong to ourselves: we were bought at a price." (1 Cor. 6:10–20)[8]

The church is a highly gifted community.

You are a highly gifted servant of the living God.

Reggie McNeal observed, "Nowhere in Scripture are we told we are going to be held accountable for talent we don't have. However, we are informed that we will be responsible for the stewardship of what we have been given. An honest assessment of talent provides an understanding of your potential and where you should be directing your energies."[9]

As stewards, we join a mission; we don't create one. We are given unique tools to show and tell of an alternative kingdom: the great kingdom of our God. God has given each of us these unique tools to retell the gospel narrative in tangible and attractive ways. We share these gifts, these tools, and these artifacts, and we can watch our culture change.[10] There is no template for how our genius can creatively tell the kingdom story, but there certainly is a calling.

DISCUSS THIS

- How do you react to the idea that *many* are a genius? Why?
- What do you believe your greatest area of creative impact is? How did you come to that conclusion?
- Describe a time when someone affirmed something specific in you. What was the result?
- How does creating bring you joy? How does it bring you stress?
- What are your greatest tools for retelling the gospel narrative in attractive ways?

CHAPTER 2

WHAT COUNTS?

Like our first parents we are to be creators
and cultivators. Or to put it more poetically,
we are to be artists and gardeners.

—Andy Crouch

He himself gives to all mankind life
and breath and everything.

—Acts 17:25

Resist the urge to feel like if it's not done for your
church or under your leadership it doesn't count.[1]

—Bob Hyatt

We *want to do something big for God in our community!"*
I started to grin as this couple in their early sixties
beamed with the passion of teenagers. John builds homes and
had just finished serving a round as mayor of their small town.
Sue has blessed countless people with her hospitality. They had
lived here for twenty-three years and seemed to know everyone.
Through work, social life, their kids' schools, and partnerships

in local organizations, they are connected. Really connected. I'm pretty sure they've had half the town around their dinner table.

They began to share how God had put a burden on them for their place, a Macedonian call of sorts. They were ready to make greater sacrifices than ever before to see the gospel wreck and rebuild the people around them. Their passion made me want to pump my fist. But I felt a twinge of something else. *Oh no!* I thought. *Have we not already allowed them to do big things for God?*

The truth is they had already been doing big things, and we all saw it. The gospel they've fleshed out is consistent and contagious. They had shepherded their town. John and Sue's story is exciting, but it's not an anomaly. There are people right under our noses who want to do something big, to take the plunge in the name of Jesus.

Every follower of Jesus who is seeking to join His mission is asking the same question. And we might be asking it with a slightly different tone and inflection. Most of us feel guilty asking it or even thinking it. Perhaps it sounds too driven, too Western, too pressurized, too human. Every mission-minded follower of Jesus is accidentally asking the question "What counts as ministry?"

Many people believe ministry is reserved for those called pastor, church leaders who talk from a stage, strike the right chords, and lead Bible studies. The term "full-time ministry" subtly functions as an offensive line, accidentally blocking many of God's people from joining God in ministry. Eugene Peterson laments how the phrase "full-time Christian work" is one of the most damaging phrases in church speak.[2]

Others believe only a few specific things count as ministry: visiting hospitals, monologuing from behind a pulpit or crossing oceans in the name of our Lord. Others think ministry is about serving on Sunday mornings or meeting the urgent call to hold babies in the nursery. The only invitation to ministry some will ever hear is "If we don't have these things in place, we can't keep all the church plates spinning!" This effectively communicates the underlying message: *If you have a pulse, we not only want you, we need you!* Even after our desperate cries we wonder why people still don't respond.

Meanwhile, there's another side of the spectrum. Some have been told they can do anything in the name of Jesus and glorify Him by doing it. MMA fight nights, pub crawls, missional coffee drinking, film screenings, and becoming a real estate tycoon sound a bit more appealing than herding cats in the children's ministry. People hear the following message: "Do everything you want to do, just do it for God. There's no need for sacrifice."

Where is the balance between these two perspectives? How can we meet needs *and* passionately live as the people God created us to be? The what-counts question has left the church largely confused about how to join God on His restorative mission to establish His kingdom reign and rule.

Every follower of Jesus has the Spirit of God within them and is given spiritual gifts. Every human is created in the image of God. I love watching people come to know Jesus and translating their gifts from secular (sometimes even selfish or shady) work into spiritual work. Some of the outputs might not change. They might continue to make lots of money, lead lots of people, create lots of change, or innovate lots of things, but their motivation begins to change.

No one feels like a genius all the time. Occasionally I feel like a genius, but usually I feel like an idiot fumbling through areas of weakness. If we aren't the best in the room, we believe we're the worst. We all have things we stumble through, feeling like we're the only one who doesn't get it. We skip over ten compliments and focus on one criticism. We crave originality and authenticity, and then we ironically copy others in our style, language, rituals, food, and relationships. We are all, somehow, completely normal yet completely original. Both sides of that coin are comforting.

Each of us has things we can do naturally, easily, effortlessly. Parker Palmer refers to our genius as our "native way of being in the world."[3] Sometimes our native abilities shine, but at other times we find ourselves feeling discouraged because we lack those abilities. We all have genius inside us. We are built to create and lead—or more accurately to co-create and co-lead.[4]

A Barber Shop at the Intersection of Two Kingdoms

Etienne went to school for computer science and accounting. After graduation, he became a CPA. He dabbled in different careers, succeeding in some, even working in a for-profit business dedicated to eradicating poverty in the third world. Then he worked in a medical device start-up that closed just a few months later. He knew he was meant for more.

After seeking God on what he should do, he couldn't shake the question: *What do you want to do?* He had diverse experiences, adequate training, and had seen a lot of the world. But he wrestled through the question, "*What do you think the world needs?*" After a month of focus, he narrowed down his list of requirements. He not only wanted to work with a team to create a profitable business, but he wanted it to intersect with his international heart. He wanted to open the global eyes of his four boys beyond vacations and mission trips. He wanted to develop people locally and across the globe.

Etienne didn't want to look back years later and regret the time he had spent at work. He wanted the line separating Jesus' mission and his daily vocation to disappear. When a barber shop was on its last leg, the owner called him and asked him to buy it. It fit all his criteria. Despite having next to no experience trimming locks, he took the plunge. Today the shop is thriving.

For Etienne, being a missionary in an entrepreneur's body can be a thankless job. He makes business decisions with Jesus' mission at the forefront. To him, his business is merely a contact point between two kingdoms. The storefront shop has become one of those special places where the veil between the two worlds can be drawn back. He mentors his employees. He has even led some folks across the line of faith. People are more important than profit, and every employee knows that. He has even forgiven debts. Like any business, there are low moments. There was the star barber who cussed him out in front of a full shop and stormed out. Twice. Eventually the man took all his clientele and their money with him.

Part of the incredible story of the shop includes a woman named Darla. Since Etienne had a total history in the hair industry of less than six months, he was desperate to find a manager with serious experience. But it wasn't easy aligning values with experience. After taking a friend's recommendation he talked to Darla for three hours. They were kindred spirits. In her thirty years in the biz, Darla had never come across anyone like Etienne who had gospel intention as his motivation. She turned down a better offer and has been managing the shop and praying for souls ever since.

Etienne and his team have even taken discipleship principles and adapted them into team mentorship principles. They have a spiritual culture in the shop. Etienne said, "I am *not* in the business of building salons or selling haircuts. I develop people, give them second chances, and shepherd people toward the kingdom of God."

He has taken a team across the globe to teach a barbershop-in-a-box training program. Over two weeks, they train barbers in some of the hardest-to-reach places and provide them with a kit that includes everything barbers need. They have been invited into several countries to do this program and are currently looking to scale their training program to wherever God wants to take it.

Etienne reminds his people, "God's work isn't always not-for-profit." He challenges every believer to listen to the Father about how they can use the skills they have. Days can have more purpose. Problems can become opportunities to build His kingdom. God has been planning our entrance to the game for longer than we've been alive. Everyone has something to offer. Everyone is unique. Everyone's a genius.

Unleashing People

I would love to see more stories like Etienne's come to life. Perhaps we've been poor storytellers. Perhaps, as church leaders, we don't have a large enough view of what vocation could look like. We have inadvertently put the genius of congregations on a leash. I confess, I'm guilty. Dogs on a leash are safe, but they usually aren't happy. We've created safe spaces for utilizing creativity within the church, but that doesn't mean we have created the right spaces. Dogs on leashes might not get hit by a car, but they also might never experience the joy of running free through a field or chasing a squirrel.

We don't mean to put people on leashes. We do it accidentally. If someone within our church has the gift of hospitality, often they feel relegated to hosting church events in their home or working in the church café. Maybe their home should become a ministry hub creating respite for the lost, lonely, and broken. Maybe instead of pouring lattes in the church café, they are supposed to start a café in the community.

It takes trust to let a dog off a leash. They trust their dog, and they are willing to take the risk to let the dog run freely.

Do you trust the people in your congregation?

Do you trust the sovereignty of God that watches, keeps, and protects them?

Do you trust people can figure it out without you or without a program?

To unleash anything requires trust. Unleashing people for the sake of the world requires us to trust God and learn to trust people. I am not saying we let people run free of any kind of accountability or free of any boundaries—in certain places and spaces invisible fencing makes sense. Everyone, especially young believers, need some boundaries or parameters. This is the act and art of discipleship. There are gray zones that are not easy to call. They require prayer and discernment.

Many of Paul's letters, especially First Corinthians, deal with living our faith with a healthy dose of cultural discernment. It would have been much easier for the apostle Paul to command the Christians in Corinth not to eat meat that has been offered to idols, drink any kind of alcohol, or exercise any kind of spiritual freedom. Legalism doesn't require discernment. A leashed congregation may be easier to lead and control, but that obsession with safety will lead a church toward a slow, safe death. Unleashing God's people and their creativity is a risk, but it's a risk we must take.

We want to change the culture of our churches, but do we want to change the culture of our cities? Perhaps our vision is too small. Perhaps our prayers are too tiny. Perhaps our desire to preserve the past in a shadow box has gotten the best of us. We need to equip and release our people for city movements. This could be a great moment. Our world is simultaneously globalizing and localizing. Social media gives us a farther reach. Civic organizations, bloggers, government offices, and clubs are recognizing people for their uniqueness. Will the church recognize the unique gifts of God's people? Will we challenge them to use those gifts to make Jesus more famous?

The church simply cannot afford to lose the influence of young and talented creatives. They are energetic and innovative and possess a different vantage of the world than any generation who has ever lived. They're not perfect, but they have potential. Yes, I believe in millennials, but we cannot afford to lose the talent and wisdom of the boomer generation. Many boomers have served in every area of our churches, from children's ministry to elder boards. They have ideas tempered with life experience, and they happen to have the money to get these ideas off the ground. People of all ages and backgrounds are waiting while their creativity sits dormant, waiting to be tapped into.

Confessions of an Accidental Creative

School was hard for me growing up. It still is. I wasn't the worst student, because I worked hard at my studies, but I wasn't the whiz kid who was celebrated on awards night. I like to move, change environments, and learn through doing. I hate wasting time on needless stuff. I was the kid who would grab the hall pass during class just to get out of my desk and walk the hallway for a few minutes. I hated to read. Why read a book when I can live a good story?

Traditional learning has never been my scene. The best thing about most conferences I attend is learning from real-life experience or escaping the event center to dream over a meal. I'm a kinesthetic, relational, experiential learner. I learn best through experience—often failure. I was never tested, but I bet they would have slapped an ADHD label on me. I have to chain myself to the desk to write a book. I have learned to temper this in myself, and I have been able to shape several learning environments for ministry that cater to folks like me who have a hard time in the classroom. Today I am glad I am built this way, but it wasn't always so.

I have never been a teacher or a school administrator, but I'm learning a lot these days. My wife and I became insta-school parents. We adopted a six-and a two-year-old and just weeks later were sitting in first grade orientation, terrified. We tried to look like we knew what we were doing. We live about a hundred yards from a school. One day I told the principal, "Just let me know how I can serve." Since then we've tried to be a support to other parents and school administrators however we can. Somehow I landed on the board that holds the administration accountable for its leadership. Not exactly my dream plan. The next year I found myself leading this team. Needless to say, I have done a lot of listening, and there is a steep learning curve.

Last year we undertook the task of completely remaking the vision, mission, and values of the school. I have always liked taking organizations and church leaders through this exercise. I met with the principal and a few high-capacity teachers. I battled with the thought, *Why am I even in this room? I don't know anything about education.* Surprisingly, the process was really fun. We asked foundational questions as I thought through a school culture that would affect my kids. It feels like I'll be an elementary school parent for eternity trapped in a cloud of teacher conferences and stupid fund-raisers. I found a longing in the administration and teachers for new forms of learning, new paradigms for education, and a broadening of the kind of students they could affect. The following are a few aims that emerged from this process:

- Grit: This matters more than traditional education has made space for. We talked through possible ways to celebrate the kid who sticks to it, not just the kid who naturally gets it.
- Risk taking: We need to find ways to celebrate the risks students take in the learning process and not create a pass-or-fail culture. Failure in public settings builds a culture of shame that causes students to seek safety rather than risk a new horizon and new discovery.
- Collaboration: School accidentally kills collaboration. "Don't look at your neighbor's paper!" combined with trying to outperform those in the desks around us creates a competitive environment instead of a collaborative spirit.

Collaborative learners contribute to healthy teams and help businesses succeed. Guarded and competitive individuals make for poor team members.

- Problem solving: Learning has been presented as cognition for sharp, quick, auditory learners instead of a space to wrestle with topics. I know I'm partial, but my daughter did the coolest science fair experiment, though she walked into the gym already knowing who the winners were going to be. We got to enjoy three types of home brewed root beer, and they got a free battery tester. Our world doesn't have clear paths and easy answers.
- Passion: We have rarely found avenues to celebrate those who are passionate about learning. The passionate will naturally apply their learning and take it beyond the walls of their classroom. I visited several zoos with my two sons this past summer. I was amazed at their passion for animals. One son spouted off facts he had learned in the classroom for every animal we saw. No one told him to learn about animals; he is just wired for it.

Once we re-formed the values, we asked the following questions:

- How will these values inform who and how we hire staff?
- How will teachers model these values in their lives?
- How will these values be applied daily in the classroom?
- How will these values be infused into the lives of the students and their families?
- How will these students carry these values with them when they leave this school?

This is the journey most organizations need to embark on. Recalibrating values, goals, and practices was exciting. Listening to teachers and refining their thoughts was educational. Metrics needed to change to celebrate new things. The questions needed to change as well.

This is exactly what the church is doing today: recalibrating. We are learning to celebrate new things and ask new questions. But we need to collaborate on a new grid for how we can more effectively celebrate, develop, and send people to inhabit and impact a changing world that is longing for meaning.

Gap Number 1: The Credibility Gap

While I sipped my coffee in my garage, I counted a pocketful of cash. I was minding my own business, sitting in my favorite lawn chair, and joyously watching people pay me to cart away my junk during a much-needed yard sale.

A man pulled up in an older Camry, pretended he was interested in my stuff, and awkwardly wandered through the junk.

What's up with this guy? I wondered. Something wasn't right. The plastic smile. The bad acting. He looked like Dwight Schrute from *The Office* meets Andy Dwire on *Parks and Recreation*.

Then he turned and suddenly approached me with the stealth of a ninja. I looked up from my wad of one dollar bills. He pulled out some literature. I was just a target. He was a Jehovah's Witness.

Most people fear similar tactics coming from evangelical Christians today. This lack of trust is referred to as the credibility gap. This gap exists because people are suspicious of followers of Jesus, believing we will beat them over their heads with the Bible or yell in their faces with a bullhorn. Those outside the church can't identify with the culture in our churches. To many folks, crossing the threshold of a church or a Christian house gathering feels like entering customs and getting your passport stamped. Many believe, even fear, every follower of Jesus is giving false love to mask what they perceive is our only motive: conversion.

Gap Number 2: The Validation Gap

I see another gap just as big, if not bigger, that is holding the church back from influence: the validation gap. We want new results in the church today, new people reached, new subcultures engaged, renewed influence on Western culture, and a blessing presence in our places. Here's the problem: on the whole we haven't shifted how we are recognizing, equipping, and releasing leaders to make an impact on the world. There's a gap between what many people hear on Sunday mornings about being an example of Jesus and how we are *actually* expecting people to join God's mission. It's as if we're doing leadership development for the church of fifty years ago. If the expectations change, so must the implications.

It's no secret people are exiting the church today. The most heartbreaking piece to me is that some of the brightest and most creative people are leaving. We haven't intentionally pushed them out; we just haven't made space for them at the table. They are gifted, and they want to lead. This is the trouble with the validation gap. Leaders lead. Influencers influence. Creatives create.

That's just how it works. If church leaders are not validating their passion and abilities, they are left with only two choices:

- Lose interest in joining God's mission but quietly reside in the pews at an emotional distance.
- Feel discontent that the things they cultivate don't "count" as God's work and make a physical exit from the church.

Emotional escape or physical escape are both bad options. If this idea of validation feels a little too theoretical for you, hold on. I promise I will flesh it out.

Leaking Creativity

Ken Robinson, a recognized expert on learning and education, places a high value on creativity. "Creativity is as important now in education as literacy, and we should treat it with the same status," he said. "Do schools kill creativity?" he asked. After years of observation he concluded: "We are educating people out of their creative capacities." Robinson believes nearly every education system today is designed solely to produce university professors.[5]

As Christian leaders, this question could translate as, *"Do churches kill creativity?"* Much of the ministry training we offer in the church is designed to produce more full-time vocational pastors. The problem is that most people don't desire this role and will never be referred to as pastors. They might shepherd people or have an amazing gospel influence, but no matter how much influence they have, they might never consider themselves church leaders.

Thus, the church is leaking creativity. It's not a burst pipe spewing gallons of water, but rather a slow drip resulting in a loss of creative pressure. And most people are sensing this loss of creative pressure. As church leaders, we have accidentally trained leaders for a small cross section of ministry tasks. When people hear the phrase "in the ministry," for most it's synonymous to a man of the cloth or a preacher. Paradoxically this has left people both disengaged and exhausted.

In her book *Multipliers*, Liz Wiseman wrote, "It is indeed possible to be both overworked and underutilized."[6] A car can overheat while only spinning its wheels in the mud. Many people in our churches are heading toward burnout in the areas they serve, but they still feel like no one has invited them to do anything challenging, exciting, or creative for the sake of the world. Their passion meter is low while their frustration meter is high.

Some family friends attended a church in our city for a while. Their church had a tradition of ending each gathering with a short time of prayer requests and opportunities. The opportunities were mostly reminders of events on the church calendar.

During one of these times, our friend stood up and shared how his family would be raking leaves that week to bless their neighbors. He invited other families from the church to join them. An awkward moment followed, and no one acknowledged this idea afterward. So my friends never took a risk to share an idea like this again.

The husband runs a successful business and advocates for humanitarian efforts. This church incident was a small, but tragic, lack of validation that led he and his family to disengage from the local church. Sadly, the only space he has found for his activism is on social media.

What if, instead, churches trained and released people back into the vocations, careers, and ideas they already have? We can make inroads to join them in their neighborhoods and in their relationships to utilize the creativity they already possess to bless the world. If we dig a little, we usually find incredible dreams and ideas for impacting people. When considering risk taking for the sake of the world, we fear rejection, but we also fear a lack of validation. Instead of sharing an idea with a church family, it's easier to share it with entrepreneurs and community leaders.

My years as a student pastor were quite a ride. Between opening an indoor skate park with no previous experience, visits to the hospital for failed suicide attempts, and going on mission with a lively leadership team, those years were full of joy, heartbreak, and surprise.

A notoriously quiet and standoffish girl—dubbed "emo" by her peers—always sat in the back during any discussion or teaching, usually leaning close to a boy. One night we asked the students to share their dreams to change the world. Emo girl lit up. She shared how the plight of orphans grieved her and how Mother Teresa was one of her heroes. She wanted to start an orphanage in India. As we prayed for students and debriefed the next morning, everyone commented on how that discussion had unlocked something inside of this quiet, withdrawn girl. Where did that come from? When invited into a bigger vision for ministry, most people will accept the invitation.

When Jesus' church is functioning as a diverse, unified, extended family on mission for the sake of the world, amazing things happen. New possibilities arise. People experience Jesus. We gain reputations as blessers in our communities.

But often we find ourselves killing a movement before it starts.

We compare our abilities to others. We look at a leader bursting with influence and wonder why we don't have that. We look at a thriving church down the road and wonder where our spark went. God did not intend for diversity to discourage but to show off His genius. The diversity of gifts and influence should remind us we are a valid, valuable part of His plan to restore all things.

Every human being possesses the divine DNA, the *imago dei*, the image of God. Alan Hirsch observed: "To believe in the imago dei is not to ignore or bypass the inherent sinfulness of all people. But it means that in spite of the fall of humankind through sin, every human being remains created and stamped with the fingerprint of God himself."[7] Our world needs God's fingerprints all over it, and God beckons us to partner with Him to infuse His love into every crack and crevice of our world.

Creativity Doesn't Have a Box

Our culture has come a long way in its view of genius. Different environments espouse different gifts, modalities, or abilities. A person's view of their own gifting is often shaped by their environment. If an environment esteems a particular ability, people in that environment will begin to believe they possess this talent. Leadership guru Max De Pree noted, "Society cultivates whatever is honored there."[8] Another way to say this is, "What gets rewarded gets done." When people find out what counts, they start doing it. That's just how it works.

I see this come to life often. Seminarians call me, usually in the winter or spring, and express an interest in coming to Colorado to start a new church. When I ask them about their gifts and abilities, nearly every time the answer is the same: teaching. This is because the gift and practice of teaching is highly esteemed in seminaries. I don't doubt these students have become strong in their public speaking ability, but I just don't think all these guys on the other end of the phone have the gift of teaching.

Some might call this a delusion, but I believe it's plain old human nature. Environments affect our self-view with subtle peer pressure, or at least a peer desire. When we focus on influencing like others do, we miss out on who God has uniquely wired us to be. It's refreshing to hear an undercurrent within the church of people realizing they are gifted in unique areas. Genius in spiritual leaders is not limited to preaching, leading mission teams, coordinating local outreach, or launching new campuses.

Genius is not just reserved for math whizzes, computer programmers, chemistry professors, novelists, or successful entrepreneurs. Someone might call you a creative genius, a social genius, an academic genius, a relational genius, a cultural genius, a historical genius, or a musical genius. The fields are expanding, which, in turn, is validating more people. This concept of multiple areas of intelligence was first introduced by Howard Gardner in 1983 in his book *Frames of Mind: The Theory of Multiple Intelligences*. One of his colleagues pointed out: "Gardner opposes the idea of labeling learners to a specific intelligence." Each individual possesses a unique blend of all the intelligences. "Gardner maintains that his theory of multiple intelligences should 'empower learners,' not restrict them to one modality of learning."[9] His thinking reminds us of the diversity of intelligence.

Gardner categorized these abilities into three overarching categories.

1. The ability to create an effective product or offer a service that is valued in a culture.
2. A set of skills that makes it possible for a person to solve problems in life.
3. The potential for finding or creating solutions for problems, which involves gathering new knowledge.

We must create more space to welcome diverse genius and intelligence to the table. When this occurs people feel empowered. We must build cultures of empowerment instead of peer-desire. Empowerment cultures celebrate diversity of genius, while peer-desire cultures envy it and snuff it out.

Kids are perhaps the easiest examples of the diversity of genius in pure form. I have four kids, and each of them shines in a different way. At a young age, you can begin to see the "it" factor, the area of life in which they have "it."

One of my kids can light up a room with his charisma. Another is musically gifted and lights up the drama stage. Another zips through homework and even solves math problems in his head for fun before bed. And another possesses humor in its most natural form. People easily recognize and comment on their talents. They are all geniuses in their own way. Our role as parents is to catch them in their genius, validate their gift, and push them toward opportunities to shine. They will struggle in areas where others are naturally gifted. There are some things they will need to work harder on than others, but my wife and I hope they will spend much of their time honing their areas of excellence and passion.

I mentioned how school was tough for me. Although I have always been a learner, I have no memories of picking up a book (in free will) to read as a kid. I had to be corralled, bribed, or "homeworked" into it. If I wanted to learn, I would ask people practical questions or work alongside someone to pick up their skills.

I will never forget the moment someone suggested my struggle with math might be a sign of a learning disability. I freaked out! The travesty of our educational processes is how genius has been sized up by IQ and corralled into test taking. No, I was not the best test taker, and sitting at a desk was not easy for me. I still struggle with it.

A Living Canvas

I will never forget the warm Virginia spring day when my dad told me I would be taking over the lawn duties. My chest puffed up a little. I mowed the grass for the first time, and I've never stopped. I became a man that day. The smell of fresh-cut grass, the patterns I could make, and the feeling of visual accomplishment echoed throughout the hallways of my soul. Grass and weeds were my medium, and a lawn mower and Weed eater were my brushes.

A neighbor asked me to mow his lawn that summer. The next summer I put flyers in mailboxes on our street and picked up more business. Every summer in high school I worked full time cutting grass, building retaining walls, staining decks, and cleaning gutters. Making money was a blast! I even employed one of my teachers, several friends, and my older brother. I still give J. R. a hard time that I was his boss. I learned a lot about leadership by running the best lawn service in town: *Al's Lawn Service—Good Service, Good Prices, Good Lookin'.* (No joke, that was actually my motto.) I couldn't wait for school to be out so I could get back to work.

Our world is becoming more diverse in the creativity we honor. We are seeing more genres of creativity validated from third-wave coffee culture to eco-enterprise to fair-trade development to social-enterprise to graphic design. Ideas are growing into prevalent subcultures. Every month I see blogs and magazines full of new businesses run by uniquely gifted leaders. The speed of innovation is racing and the scope of creativity is broadening. Is the culture of our churches going to grow and expand too?

DISCUSS THIS

- In your ministry environment, what things "count" as ministry? How has your answer to this changed over the last few years?
- Do you feel leashed or free to do ministry? Why?
- Do you believe those you lead feel leashed or free? Why?
- Where is the greatest creative leak in your church or ministry? How did this develop?
- Describe the practices in your church or ministry for recognizing and affirming creativity in others. What practices can you add?
- Does your church or ministry have more of a peer-desire culture or an empowerment culture? How did this develop?

CHAPTER 3

CREATIVE ESPIONAGE

It is likely that art was the first of the human professions.
—Paul Johnson

No one is a genius all the time. . . .
But all of us are geniuses sometimes.
—Seth Godin

Christians work and live in every walk of life,
every vocation, and at every level of education, and,
therefore, the church permeates all sectors of culture.[1]
—Kevin Palau

Simon sat with me over a cup of locally roasted coffee and processed how he got from somewhere to here. He found himself immersed in creative environments as a kid. He was interested in music and production. He started hanging out at studios with bands and getting into recording and mixing. He picked up an interest in photography from his mom. A friend had a video camera and an editing system, which intrigued him. They started making goofy videos. Over time, he and his friend started producing videos for his dad's business. After recording a football game and editing it, he landed a paid gig editing game films for other teams in the city.

At seventeen, Simon went on a trip to a Russian orphanage. His heart broke. It was one of the most significant experiences of his life. He chronicled his season working at a summer camp at the orphanage. At the end of the trip, the team had to say good-bye to the kids. He filmed the grit and tears of the long good-bye. It wrecked him. He edited the footage of the trip and told the story in fifteen minutes of video. The slow-motion shots tattooed images onto the minds of viewers.

Suddenly Simon's dabbling with camera work became something special. He was able to transport people who hadn't been on the trip to feel what he felt and experience what he had experienced. He watched his videos make an impact. He connected people to a new story through the medium of film. He pulled them into a story they had not and perhaps would never experience. "How was your trip?" suddenly made sense to people.

Two years later, Simon returned to Russia to find a different scene in the orphanage. It was cold. There were no other groups leading camp. Laughs no longer echoed down the hallways. This time he produced a script to accompany the footage. Hundreds watched the short film and were exposed to the real story of Russian orphans.

He wanted to affect people through film for a living. Months later a producer validated his potential. Simon showed a raw, grainy film to a production manager in hopes of landing an internship. She saw something in Simon. He possessed raw skill that is hard to teach and goes beyond the technical elements students learn in film school. Simon knew how to capture a story. He possessed something innately, but he needed an opportunity. They took a chance on him. Instead of an offer, he received an invitation. They invited him to show up without a job, hang around the office, and learn from the team. So he showed up, learned, and looked for opportunities. He loved it. It lit him up. They gave him affirmation and access.

Simon peeked into the world of professional filmmaking and found himself in an unexpected apprenticeship. Eventually he had a shot at a small role in a big project. He started getting paying jobs. One leader giving him one small opportunity catapulted Simon into a future of changing the world. Simon said: "They saw something in me that I didn't see in myself. What a gift they gave me."

Today, Simon is a documentary filmmaker. He gets to amplify voices in the world who need to be heard. He exposes causes that need to be championed from orphan care to sex trafficking to global poverty to economics.

Perhaps the greatest gift Simon is giving others is education. He tells stories people need to hear. He brings awareness to major issues by bringing stories from the margins to the center of our attention. He is careful not to shock people or exploit others for a good cause. He takes his craft and his gift seriously.

Simon connects deeply with the people he interviews as he captures glimpses of their story. He cares deeply. His films create connections between people. He's not just a storyteller or a filmmaker; he's a connector of human hearts. He is a dealer of meaning. Humans aren't props or even propagators; they are creative, valuable beings.

What is Simon's motivation? He is digging below the surface to find value in people who are created in the image and likeness of God.

People want to have an impact on the world. We are hungry to create meaning and utilize our careers to make a difference. A recent study reveals that more than a third of millennials expect to make an impact through their work within the first five years.

Younger leaders have a desire to accumulate meaning, not just wealth.[2] Preston Sprinkle noted, "Churches can nurture this passion and help Millennials stay connected to Christ by focusing on vocational calling outside of traditional church-based ministry."[3] How can churches do this? Church leaders can affirm and fan creative and altruistic flames, but we must become spies in order to do so. We need to watch others closely, trying to spy their genius.

Unearthing Things in Others

When I was a kid, I spent a lot of time with a shovel in my hand. I dreamed of digging up an ancient city or dinosaur bones. I even tried to dig and get to China. One day I learned about gold at school. After the bell rang I came home and started to excavate. My shovel became my tool. A few days later I finally found some. From the hard Virginia clay, I unearthed a chunk of (fool's) gold. After digging around it and lifting it out with all my might, I ran to show my mom the treasure. She told me it wasn't real. Obviously, she was no prospector.

Christian leaders wield a shovel. We must become archaeologists seeking to uncover the precious gifts buried below the surface in those around us. Sometimes the ground is hard and requires a pickax to start to unearth the shimmer of something beautiful inside others. It can be hard, slow work, but it's worth it.

As church leaders, we often become so focused on dictating things to our people that we don't take time to unearth and uncover their unique fingerprint and creative makeup. There is a space inside all of us where the image of the Creator rises to the surface. Sometimes we do things both naturally and skillfully, and it even blows us away.

One year a winsome couple went through a learning track I led. When we started the journey, they were considering leaving their church, joining a church start-up, or launching into global missions. The husband seemed antsy, ready to delve into a new avenue to serve God. After a few sessions, they began to invite people to their home for lunch. Many of our young single leaders were more than happy to consume their homemade cuisine. The group would spend hours in their home with their family, eating and talking about the ups and downs of life. One snowy Saturday my family joined the group for some hot soup next to a fire as we consumed their amazing hospitality.

During their commissioning time, we all recounted stories of moments in their home. For the previous ten months they had cracked open their lives and invited us in. God used this time to shift their trajectory from what they *wanted to be doing* toward what they were *already doing* effectively. We clearly communicated to them: *this hospitality counts as ministry!* You don't have to do anything else. Just keep doing what you're doing!

How many people around us are just like this couple? How many people are aspiring to find an area of greater impact while they are already making a big impact?

If you are a Christian leader, you need to function as a creative spy and a human archaeologist. We should constantly be following the trail of creativity in others and affirming what we find in them. The fourth chapter of Ephesians talks about some crucial but different wirings of Christian leaders. Apostolic, prophetic, evangelistic, shepherding, and teaching wirings are not just for the sake of infusing those in the church; they are also for recognizing and equipping others to function in these ways. We are "to equip the saints for the work of ministry, for building up the body of Christ."[4]

Multiplication cannot truly happen until we are recognizing, validating, and equipping others. A mature body of Christ will impact families, neighborhoods, cities, and the world. The church also cannot grow into maturity until we take responsibility for recognizing and equipping others.

Church leaders, we aren't the apex of the story. Our lives should extend to recognize and release others into a world desperately needing to experience the genius God has planted in us all. Liz Wiseman, author of *Multipliers,* said, "At the top of the intelligence hierarchy is not the genius but the genius-maker."[5] The true work of ministry is not found in developing our gifts but in developing the gifts of those around us. Look for the genius in others.

How do we balance the reality that everyone *is* a genius while reminding them it's only because they *have* genius?

How do we recognize and affirm those we lead without creating a prideful culture?

Here is a diagram that has been incredibly helpful for me as I lead others and try to recognize this in myself.

The Spectrum of Recognition

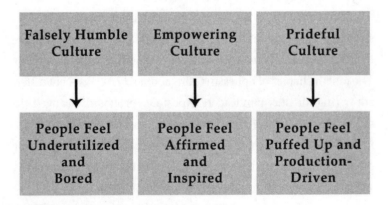

Falsely Humble Culture	Empowering Culture	Prideful Culture
↓	↓	↓
People Feel Underutilized and Bored	People Feel Affirmed and Inspired	People Feel Puffed Up and Production-Driven

The Balance of Recognition

Every church and organization must find a balance of recognition. As the diagram shows, there are two ways we can go off the tracks and fall into the ditch.

Falsely Humble Culture

A falsely humble culture is largely a reaction against a culture of over-recognition and pride. Instead of looking to discover and recognize the gifts latent in people, the leaders steer away from anything that can be perceived as pride in one's abilities. While sensitivity to pride and ambition is necessary, this culture overcorrects and stifles people from leading from their gifts or wiring, as Scripture talks about.

In these cultures, very few people have meaningful roles, and the search for excellence has been abandoned before it even began. In a church with a falsely humble culture, the people are underutilized and bored. This culture fails to recognize, raise up, and multiply leaders. Passive leaders wait for a pastor to dictate the next series, idea, or initiative to the church body. This culture will subtly suck the life out of people or, at the least, their creativity.

Prideful Culture

A prideful leadership culture is on the opposite end of the spectrum. The leaders at the top are highly valued for what they do and for their talents. Those newly assembled into the mix wonder where they will shine and how they can serve in the areas that are touted as important. When people fill spots of importance, they are treated with greater respect.

When you peer into this culture, you can immediately feel

the pressure to produce, to be known, to be validated, and to create a better experience than the last time. While a culture of excellence is certainly not a bad thing, an obsession with excellence raises the bar so high it only validates the excellent ones. This will produce pride in some and shame in others and ultimately results in a production-driven attitude. This culture tends to burn through leaders quickly.

Empowering Culture

Sitting in tension between these two ditches we find an empowering culture. The first thing this culture validates is God's role as Creator and Author. The second thing this culture validates is that every human being is stamped with God's image and is valuable as His child. This gives people freedom to take risks, to exercise their gifts, and to be seen as creative and unique. People feel empowered and excited that they get to partner with God in ministry. They feel inspired to find where they fit in and where they can serve.

Validating cultures are always seeking to find new ways to affirm people. At the beginning of each school year, a church in my city gets everyone in public education—teachers, administrators, and even groundskeepers—onstage and commissions them as missionaries into the public schools. Not only do those leaders feel validated, but everyone in the room gets the picture that their work matters. Another church acknowledges everyone in the church is a missionary cleverly disguised as a businesswoman, a firefighter, or a lawyer.

It is crucial to build a culture of empowerment in churches if we are going to see missionaries released to join the great missionary in His work. The word *empower* has three important definitions:[6]

1. "to give official authority or legal power to"

    In the truest sense, God has already granted this to every believer. Everyone who is part of God's family has the authority of the Father. In the Great Commission, Jesus starts with the power that has been vested in Him ("All authority in heaven and on earth has been given to me"—Matt. 28:18), and He transfers that authority to the disciples and to all the disciples that will come later ("Go therefore and make disciples"—verse 19).

    - "All authority in heaven and on earth has been given to me": God the Father gave Jesus the authority.
    - "Go therefore": Jesus transfers that authority to the disciples.
    - "make disciples . . . baptizing them . . . teaching them": Every follower of Jesus is empowered with authority.

    At times, we will need to follow Jesus' example and give a similar transfer of authority. At times, we need to extend official permission to lead within our organization or church. Those who feel they are not allowed to lead are living in a form of poverty. Andy Crouch noted, "Poverty is not just a matter of lacking financial resources; it can also simply mean being cut off from cultural power."[7] Encouraging others to use their God-given abilities is a way of reminding them of the power God has given us all.

2. "to enable"

    The second definition speaks about permission. God has made serving possible by creating us in His image, and each of us is endowed with unique talents. While God initiates the ability to join His mission, we function as part of God's enabling process of giving others permission to serve. Sometimes this feels strange, more like validation than permission, but we are certainly called to participate.

3. "to promote the self-actualization or influence of"

This definition is where we, as God's people, are crucial. We don't create people or embed their uniqueness; God does. We don't give the official power to do work in God's name; Jesus did. We do, however, "promote the self-actualization or influence of" those around us. We help others unearth what is already there, to actualize. We help people make sense of where they are unique and how that uniqueness can be both an act of worship and a blessing to others. When we empower people, we don't give them the power or the abilities, but we remind them of the authority and abilities God has already given them.

Recently I was privileged to spend a few days learning at the feet of Eugene Peterson and his wonderful wife, Jan. A few of us sat in the Petersons' living room enjoying muffins, sipping coffee, and looking out at beautiful Flathead Lake. We felt welcome from the moment we entered their home.

Jan reflected on how it took her many years to uncover her hospitality gift. "I had always practiced hospitality," she said, "but I never realized it was truly part of me." For three years their church gathered in their basement, and she played host at countless events, Bible studies, and last-minute meetings. I'm sure others spotted the gift during her early years of ministry, but no one pulled her aside and let her know how truly special that was. What if someone had taken the time to affirm her in that gift and encourage her to practice it more?

Empowerment has a crucial partner. We can't forget to have fun as we develop teams. Creativity thrives when we're having fun. It spices up meetings and gatherings. Add a dose of fun to the batch as you develop people.

Often I watch my kids make swords out of croquet mallets, build little houses with bricks, or play in our garden bed. The key is my wife and I have to say, "Turn off the TV and go outside and play" for them to start playing and start creating. Play starts with an invitation.

Have a leadership meeting around a fire pit after a make-your-own pizza dinner. Start with a fun game. Play "would you rather?" or "two truths and a lie." Bring your favorite breakfast to start a meeting. Get out of the office and walk and talk when you meet with someone. Give people permission to laugh at themselves and others on the team. Empowerment not only gives permission to lead and take risks but permission to have fun while you're doing it.

Scouting for Talent

A wise sage has taught me a lot about spying for talent. As his kids were growing up, he and his wife put a high priority on watching them when they didn't know it, spying on them. They would try to catch them in their element in moments of focus. He saw amazement in his son when he stared into their fish tank. He watched him at the zoo trying to figure out how those exotic animals could move like they do. Although he knew next to nothing about biology, he would take his son to pet stores and encourage him to take challenging biology classes in high school. He recognized his son had an unquenchable fire for observing bodies in motion. Today his son is a chiropractor who helps people understand the needs of their bodies and how they can recover from pain. His four kids are firmly planted in very diverse careers they deeply love.

- Are you studying those you lead?
- Are you scouting the people in the congregation or in the circle around you for talent?
- Be students of those around you to discover their hopes, hurts, and history.[8]

Focus on being interested instead of interesting. There's always one person at the table who wants to share how interesting they are, tell you all the places they've been, list all the people they've rubbed shoulders with, and subtly mention all their accomplishments. Ain't nobody got time for the #humblebrag. I like to sit next to the person who asks questions, the one who truly wants to know how you are and who you are. The irony is that these folks are the most interesting ones at the table.

Many innovators—people we might call world changers— were discovered when someone recognized something remarkable in them when they were young. Those who were bold enough to validate them also challenged them, inspired them, invested in them, made a way for them to attend a formative experience, or even funded one of their projects. They recognized something in them and validated it.

Make it a habit to set a close watch on those around you and look for their unique genius. Instead of seeking to place people in an open position, what if we waited a bit and just watched them?

What people naturally get excited about says a lot about them. Pay attention to what they laugh about and cry about. Social media, visits to their home, and asking intentional questions are great ways to dig a little deeper. Find out what they do on their days off and what they are skipping church services to do. Look beyond church attendance (or lack thereof) to find what their hearts beat for, what they do in their free time, their hobbies, and their family rhythms to see what truly makes them tick.

It's also important for people to know their church leaders have lives, priorities, and hobbies too. Don't feel pressured to always welcome people into formal positions in your church. What if we could validate the things people are already doing effortlessly and channel them toward doing them more intentionally?

We want to reach people no one else is reaching. But to do this, we have to mobilize different types of people and validate different ways of reaching people. People most naturally reach others they can identify with. For this reason, I recommend people get connected to churches in my city full of bikers, skaters, internationals, those in recovery, and ex-gang bangers, because certain churches bear unique marks. We must get a vantage bigger than our own church. We must have a vantage to see our whole city.

We are in the age of crowdsourcing and crowdfunding. More people are giving to new projects and ideas than ever before thanks to websites like Indiegogo and Kickstarter. Since 2009, more than $1.6 billion has been pledged by 8.3 million people to 82,000 different projects on kickstarter.com, the most well-known crowdsourcing website. Every month more than 15 million people from 224 countries visit Indiegogo.[9] More crowdsourcing options are popping up all the time.

Every initiative someone launches on these sites started as a simple idea, but with perseverance and some vision casting, these ideas became realities. Like it or not, we live in a crowdsourced world today. The church should be the greatest crowdsourcing engine on the planet. Are we inspiring people to engage the needs, desires, and opportunities of the day?

Validating Creativity

We all need validation. Yes, all of us. I don't care how confident you appear or how skilled you are. The need for validation is buried deep in the human heart. Validation conveys, "You are valuable. What you are doing is valid and worth your time. You are someone worth celebrating as well as someone who can do something worth celebrating."

Once we discover genius in others, we must validate it. Validation yields affirmation and celebration. Every human being longs to be celebrated. Validating someone, especially for something they didn't know was valuable, is a game changer. It calls out something good and calls them up to the level of stewardship and responsibility.

Those we might call world changers often reference a time when a teacher, parent, or mentor saw something special in them. While I experienced the disappointment of not winning the science fair in fourth grade and not getting into the starting lineup on my basketball team in tenth grade, I also remember receiving an award for character that reminded me that it counted. What people are celebrated for, positively or negatively, will stamp their souls.

The people of Jesus should become masters at helping others discover who they are, what they are gifted at, and how this could bless the world. In my experience, the hardest things for people to see are the things deep within themselves that our culture does not cheer for. When people get inklings of who they are, they begin to wonder how they can take it to a larger scale. We wonder things like, *How can this ability influence others? How can I creatively bless the world? How could this ability trampoline out of the walls of the church and make a splash in the community?*

Natural creativity is what we are looking for. Liz Wiseman describes this as "a natural ability—something that I did both easily and freely."[10] These are native abilities; things people do without being asked and without being paid.[11] Followers of Jesus need to become what Wiseman refers to as "talent magnets." These folks shape a culture of sending and releasing individuals to travel the road toward confident practice.[12] Talent magnets not only recognize and attract talent, they challenge others to take it to significant spaces of influence.[13]

When something comes naturally to us, we often wonder, *Why can't everyone do this?* My wife often lovingly reminds me, "The world is not like you." We often assume what comes naturally to us should be natural for everyone. This is also true when I struggle to do things that come naturally to others. Kids understand native abilities. They will say, "Watch this," before they attempt something. It's as if they're saying, "I'm about to do something awesome, and you don't want to miss it!"

We all must take the treacherous journey to finding our own voice. Genius cannot and should not be compared. Authors and speakers need to find *their voice*. Basketball players need to find *their game*. Runners need to run *their race* at *their pace*. Artists need to find *their style*. Pastors need to learn to pastor *their congregation*.

But why are these things theirs? Not because they created

these, but because God entrusted these to them. Comparison wrecks genius and kills joy. Jenni Catron observed, "We should be comparing ourselves only to our God-given potential."[14] We all must take the journey to find our own voices, learning to trust the One who created us every terrifying step of the way.

DISCUSS THIS

- Is your ministry environment falsely humble, prideful, or empowering? What are the indicators?
- In which ways are you inspiring others to engage the needs, desires, and opportunities around them?
- What practices do you have for studying and affirming those around you?
- What practices do you have for developing the gifts of those around you?
- In what ways do you transfer authority to those you lead? How does this affect them?

CHAPTER 4

THE NEW GENIUSES

Some organizations haven't realized this yet, or
haven't articulated it, but we need artists.[1]
—Seth Godin

The Bible makes it clear that every time
there is a story of faith, it is completely
original. God's creative genius is endless.
—Eugene H. Peterson

The only way to create culture is to make more of it.[2]
—Andy Crouch

Dan was always making things as a kid. He loved to tinker, to try to make things better. He was always fascinated by his dad's old leather bag. The leather was worn like Grandpa's favorite easy chair next to the wood stove. It mesmerized him. He was amazed it was still as strong as it was the day it was made. The bag had endless tales to tell of business trips, important presentations, and exciting adventures.

This fascination led Dan to work with leather. He sells his

goods all over the world. People crave that personal touch of knowing who made their product with their own hands. There's something divinely earthy about knowing a living, breathing human being made it. It's personal. Love and care are the two main ingredients.

Dan's craft has connected him to many people and built countless bridges for him. As a craftsman, he has common ground. He listens to the stories of other makers, and he shares his.

He feels a deep sense of accomplishment when he makes something, an identification with God's stamp of approval: "this is good." The Creator Himself marveled at His handiwork, just as Dan marvels at his. We need not only allow but also encourage people to be creative and give them opportunities to create.

Dan reminds us we serve the most creative being in the universe: the living God. He crafted us in His image. He created us to create. I failed to mention Dan is also a pastor. Many would resist opening up to Dan the pastor, but they are ready to interact with Dan the craftsman, Dan the artist, Dan the creative. Our creativity makes us distinct to the core. It also makes us and the gospel we carry accessible to others.

Do Good Work

Every human being is wired to make changes, to lead a movement, no matter how small his or her contribution might be. Ephesians 2:10 reminds us God has prepared "good works" for us. Making a mark on the world is a longing of the human heart. And God intended it to be that way.

Authenticity is crucial to both creativity and ministry.[3] Our world craves authenticity, but few believe it can be found in the church. Artists, leaders, creatives, and disciple makers must fight for authenticity, not for the sake of individuality, but for the sake of freedom and impact. We must recover both a creative and authentic witness in the world. What we create makes us authentic. The church is a people who meaningfully and authentically work. Being the church—as Christ intended us to be—takes work. Work gets a bad rap, but we're made for meaningful work. I see the church is recovering these three forms of work.

The Good Work of Hospitality

Hospitality builds beautiful bridges to authenticity. The best meetings and conversations happen over good food and good drink, but at its core hospitality is more about an open life than a full table. Having the hospitality of an open life will take work and sacrifice. Hospitality literally sets the table for conversation, prayer, and dreams. Prepare coffee for a friend, invite a neighbor into your messy life, or put away your phone as you listen intently.

The Good Work of Liturgy

"The term *liturgy* comes from two Greek works, *laos* and *ergon,* meaning 'people' and 'work.'"[4] In its truest form, the liturgy of church gatherings is a microliturgy that propels us into the macroliturgy of work amid the glory of God. Part of the liturgy of our church includes a sending at the end of the service that reminds us we are a sent people. Communion reminds us the center of our lives is not our own work, but the finished work of Christ. Submitting to sabbath forms a liturgy of rest spanning 14 percent of our time on earth. Microliturgy shapes macroliturgy. The statements we repeat and the rhythms we complete ready us for reentry into God's kingdom work.

The Good Work of Our Hands

The great C. S. Lewis pointed out the crucial difference between "good works" and "good work." He said,

> "Good works" in the plural is an expression much more familiar to modern Christendom than "good work." Good works are chiefly almsgiving and "helping" in the parish. The apostle Paul says everyone must not only work but work to produce what is "good." The idea of "good work" is not quite extinct among us, though it is not, I fear, especially characteristic of religious people. I have found it among cabinetmakers, cobblers, and sailors. . . . Artists also talk of "good work"; but decreasingly. They gain to prefer words like "significant," "important," "contemporary," or "daring."[5]

Lewis found the ethic of good work alive and well among the makers of his day, and his words can be a warning to us: be careful devaluing good work simply because we don't recognize it as good works. We generally understand the idea of good works today as helping those in tangible need and serving the least and the lost. These were hugely important to Jesus and should be hugely important to us. But we must rediscover the practical theology of good work.

The new geniuses are applying themselves to areas they are passionate about. Geniuses like Dan are hard at work in a shop, a studio, a program, or a relationship, doing what they are wired to do. Professor Teresa Amabile observed, "People will be most creative when they feel motivated primarily by the interest, satisfaction, and challenge of the work itself—and not by external pressures."[6]

True creativity is tethered to authenticity. Our motivation to create is not self-induced; it is a divine breeze blowing through us. We have the Spirit of God running through our veins, bringing us joy in this privilege; we *get* to create.

Look Out for Artists!

Artists are the sleeping giants within our churches. By nature, right brainers are hard to corral. They don't fit in a box. They don't even care a box exists. Seth Godin noted: "The reason that art (writing, engaging, leading, all of it) is valuable is precisely why I can't tell you how to do it. If there were a map, there'd be no art."[7] Artists are all around you, but you might not see them. They are subtly making beauty, telling truth, and creating subversive movements.

My friend Bryson is a wildly talented musician. The first time I met him in a coffee shop, I could tell he was talented. There's something about the way a true musician speaks intimately of a tune. They speak of their instrument like my grandfather spoke of his wartime friends. On the spot, I invited him to wrangle some musicians for a basement concert two nights later. In the catacombs of our basement his musical genius escaped. I closed my eyes, and my soul took it all in. Since that day, I have watched him take his faith, his family, and his craft seriously. Here's what Bryson said about the importance of recognizing and empowering the artists in your city.

The artists among you are the storytellers, the dreamers, the ones in the sky who can see ahead. Artists are the prophetic voice of a city. This goes for those who follow Jesus or those who don't. They are the barometer for change in communities. They make tangible the future reality of their city through art. I believe one of the church's primary responsibilities for their city is to witness their city's artists, honor their travailing voice of change, and pull out the gospel threads in their work. The church must honor, respect, and pay attention to the voice of their culture, especially when artists in your city are harmonizing with kingdom melodies.

Those are profound words. Artists carry powerful potential that is often unrecognized by the church. We must be scouting for talent in new areas. Church leaders must be looking for new geniuses.

Alternative Creatives

In his book *Linchpin*, Seth Godin wrote, "Most artists can't draw.... But all artists can see."[8] The following types of people are "see-ers," people with vision about what the world could be. We need to keep an eye out to recognize the creativity of God's people, validate it, and challenge them to be released and bless the world with it.

They are among us, and they are incredibly talented, but we usually don't see their value. We need to start spying for these people and helping them recognize how valuable they can be to the work of the kingdom. These are in no particular order.

Handcrafters

During the Renaissance there were guilds, support groups, and collaborative networks of artists and makers. Today we are moving back to a culture of makers. In a mass-produced Walmart and Ikea world, people are longing for locally sourced goods made with labor and love.

The North American church is teeming with people who are making incredible things out of wood, stone, earth, and metal. Perhaps some of them have been asked to build sets for a church stage or create a piece to hang in their church, but if we're honest, this is often boring for them. They want to be validated in how they are creating things in secular spaces. The sky is the limit for these folks from woodworking to painting to glassblowing to jewelry to roasting coffee to leather goods.

Conveners

These folks have probably invited you to a party or you've heard about their gatherings. One of the greatest things followers of Jesus should focus on is making a scene for Jesus that invites others to peer at Him. This often looks like a party, but it could be intentional community discussions, BBQs, concerts, neighborhood gatherings, school functions, small groups busting at the seams, or book clubs.

Conveners love to gather the right groups of people, and they do it naturally. Perhaps they don't even know this is a gift and might never have had someone affirm how making a scene can create kingdom mischief. You might spy them planning events, curating art shows, planning dinner parties, or taking charge of company gatherings.

Caregivers

This is perhaps the most tangible way anyone can show care for someone else: care for their physical body during a time of distress. Caregivers are the ones who procure Tylenol for someone with a headache or respond immediately when someone passes out. They notice the chronic needs of the sick, suffering, and elderly and sit as companions in their pain. They physically and tangibly show care to those in need, and they thrive in situations where people are suffering or are in pain.

Hospitables

These folks have a way of making everyone feel comfortable. I love being around these people, and I especially love entering a relaxing space they've prepared or enjoying food they've cooked. These folks serve others by making them feel comfortable, well-fed, and relaxed.

My friend Trevor cooked in restaurants for years, and his love for cooking is irrepressible. Watching him in a kitchen puts me at ease. He cooks gourmet food for large groups without stress. Through the grease and the steam, he emerges victorious against any food. I have planned several events where the food quality was hugely important. Every time, Trevor rose to the occasion. I could sit with friends, be fully present, enjoy amazing cuisine, and say thank-you to friends while he took care of the cuisine.

Feeding others is a great way to show hospitality, but it's not the only way. Being a hospitable isn't always about the food; it's about having an open life. My wife doesn't love to cook, but loves to open her life to others. Biblical hospitality is about opening your life to outsiders, not simply hosting Bible study groups in a clean home with good food on the table. Folks who are wired this way might desire to open their home to children through foster care, become a chef, host neighbors, or pursue interior design.

Experimentalists

Some people have a gift for trying anything. Yes, I think some have a natural bent and personality to try an idea on the edge of failure with no idea whether it will fly. They get a rush from it. As you can imagine, they are high on the faith spectrum. They are likely to lean into a challenging environment and be *excited* that those before them have failed and the odds seem nearly impossible. They might have a few ideas that don't work en route to the big one that does.

Some may perceive them as failures, because things haven't always worked out. But their optimism always brings others around to partner with them in their next idea. History is full of failures who eventually succeeded. Often these folks are serial entrepreneurs.

Processors

These folks are amazing at analyzing an idea or process and making it better. They want to poke something and make it stronger. They aren't out to crush the ideas or dreams of others, but to be a necessary piece of a developing puzzle. These folks have been invaluable to me when I've asked for their discernment on one of my (usually crazy) ideas. They bring wisdom that would have taken months or years in the trenches to learn. These folks can save us a lot of heartache. Whether they are ever called *consultants*, this is the role they play for those around them. They make other people more effective.

Storytellers

These people bring entertainment and meaning to the people around them. We can observe the same story unfold in a different context, and somehow it didn't seem so funny, so entertaining, or so meaningful as it does when a storyteller presents it. They translate meaning through their stories. They have practiced their whole lives around campfires and in living rooms, but most storytellers have never been challenged to bring good to the world through their stories. These folks might head toward the film industry, write for a living, create comic relief in meetings or raise awareness for nonprofits.

Cultural Translators

These people are always looking for meaningful metaphors, ideas, or themes within the culture that shed light on a deeper truth. They watch a movie, listen to a song, or digest an article and somehow relate it to another area of life. They translate how words, images, and ideas apply to the human experience. Something clicks when they share it, something we never quite thought of that way. They are always seeking to unearth meaning.

Questioners

We want these people across the table from us. They genuinely care. They have a way of actively listening and asking piercing questions that get into our bloodstream and keep us up at night. They give us their full attention and have a way of unlocking things inside us that we didn't have the key to. They pose crucial questions that we didn't even know we wanted to ask.

Ritualists

These people bring extraordinary meaning to ordinary events. They create ceremonies and know how to make a moment special. They can turn a meal or a social gathering into a meaningful and unforgettable event. They can plan a ceremony when everyone else just wants to look at their phones. They uncover, create, and repeat meaningful life practices that bring people together. They create liturgy for life.

Justice Seekers

These people call us to testify. They are passionate about causes, and their passion is convicting. They are infectious, reminding us to look below the surface and fight for the least, the lost, and the last. They bleed for others, and their passion allows them to sell ice to Eskimos. Their convictions run deep, and they know how to prick our conscience. They might be raising awareness for a cause or speaking for an organization, but after they speak, we find ourselves drawn to participate and yearning to change the world.

Wordsmiths

These folks whisper truth in beautiful ways. They have a gift for writing, speaking, and singing phrases that stick in our brains and hearts. They make others think of the world in a new way, and they have a knack for doing this beautifully. They are gentle prophets who woo us into thinking and living differently. They might be writing poetry, songs, or blogs with a particular artistry. Wordsmiths are sages who go to war with strings, phrases, harmonies, rhymes, and experiences.

Sorters

These folks are amazing at processing information and sorting it into useful categories. While we might find ourselves staring at data for a long time, they can analyze the data and put the pieces together quickly. Sorters have an incredible ability to scan information and inform groups to accomplish the next necessary steps.

These folks naturally find themselves as project managers leading a team down some peculiar alleyways where they will accomplish crucial steps. These folks are invaluable behind the scenes and rarely get overwhelmed. They keep organizations from getting bogged down in the details.

Conversationalists

Somehow these folks can make a meaningful conversation out of any subject. They can approach a topic, issue, or idea ready to learn and able to apply their knowledge in clear, precise ways. They are skilled at talking about difficult topics in approachable ways. These folks might invite us to coffee to talk about the latest issues in politics or just to shoot the breeze, but somehow they are able to take the conversation somewhere deeper than we had imagined.

Marketeers

These folks enjoy identifying and selling products or services. They are built to expose us to goods or services in ways that don't seem forced or manipulative. They market through relationships. They are evangelists for things that can meet a need and fill a niche, and we are inclined to believe them.

Story Catchers

These folks don't write good stories; they catch them. They find what is unfolding in the world that is worth reframing and translate it for us. They often champion a cause by exposing injustice or beauty or both. These folks might produce documentaries, look for stories of change from the impact of an organization, edit publications, or host podcasts.

Technologists

They see the possibilities technology offers us. They find or create technology to meet a distinct need in the world. If it doesn't exist, they think through the tools it takes to meet the need and simplify the process. We find ourselves going to these folks when we seem to be fighting against technology, and we know there ought to be an app for this. To them, innovation is deeply practical and even simple. They apply technology to real-life issues.

Connectors

These folks connect us to the others we need to know. They are enamored by the power and potential of connecting people in order to find deeper impact. Seven degrees of separation? No way. They seem to have only one or two degrees of separation to anyone on the planet.

They listen to our problems and think of the right person they can connect us with in order to take us to the next level. They show great value to us by leveraging their relationships to help make us more effective. These folks are key to the network-centric world in which we live. They help us unlock great possibilities.

Engaging Causes

Causes are a big deal today. Advocacy is on the rise. People seem compelled to make a difference and change the world. When we tap into one of these areas, we know it, because we've hit a land-mine of passion. They deeply matter to our society as a whole and to those around us.

Preston Sprinkle observed: "The church has done a poor job at thoughtfully engaging the pressing issues of the day. From science to sexuality, Christians are being told what to think, not how to think."[9] We need people who will thoughtfully engage in the areas the gospel beckons us to talk about, preach about, act on, and advocate for.

Causes hit nerves in our humanity. They can become common connectors between a church and their community. When the church champions things the community already cares about, beautiful things unfold. These can range from a passion for an international fair trade to public health development to environmental issues to orphan care to neighboring to empowering local businesses. (See the appendix of Potential Causes to Champion at the back of the book for an extensive list.)

Genius Ninjas

Geniuses are like ninjas. No, they're not lurking in the bushes ready to mess you up; they're quietly massaging the gospel into their places. They aren't preoccupied with drawing attention to themselves; they are faithfully developing others in the name of Jesus. One of my favorite developing stories has been slowly germinating in Omaha for nearly four decades.

This past summer I took a monster road trip with my two sons. We dropped into various communities along the way to see firsthand what God was up to. I dialogued with different groups and listened a lot. It was an incredible field trip! Omaha was one of our favorite stops. In just a few days we experienced the divisions, joy, heartbreak, crime, beauty, food, realities, and the amazing people of Omaha. Two of those people are Ron and Twany Dotzler.

God met Ron and Twany in the fears of inner-city life in North Omaha many years ago. When Ron looked back, he said, "While I imagined God using me to transform the brokenness of the inner city, God was actually using the brokenness of the inner city to transform me."[10] They didn't live in a dream neighborhood with a white picket fence but in one of the worst sectors of the murder map of the city. Ron and Twany wanted to run from the realities of the inner city for the sake of their kids, but God reminded them the gospel is not convenient, but it's worth it. So they raised fourteen kids (not a misprint) amid these realities, training them for lives of ministry through gospel immersion.

Long before equipping and releasing others into North Omaha, God released Ron with this call:

> My plea for pastors is to reconnect the church to the city. This call to action goes beyond churches simply giving money to foreign missions and local nonprofit ministries. Giving money without regularly giving our time to areas of need within our communities wedges distance between the churched and the unchurched. Christians need to personally connect with brokenness to connect with God's heart. When we are broken over what breaks God's heart, passion compels us to action.[11]

I love that call to action! It's compassion that drives us into our communities and away from comfort, not just our desire to utilize our gifting. We are given gifts so we can give them away, but it starts with a posture of love.

Ron believes the good work of loving our neighbors has to be connected to the local church. God used Ron, Twany, and others in North Omaha to found Abide Ministries and Bridge Church to love and serve the city from the inside out. They have even placed so-called lighthouses in troubled and dangerous neighborhoods, where families move into the neighborhoods to tangibly show the love of Jesus. Hearts have changed. Neighborhoods have changed. North Omaha has changed.

Today Ron continues to serve with Abide and plays a coaching role for the next generation of church leaders in Omaha. He discipled and developed my friend, Myron, into an amazing pastor and church planter. Ron took in Myron during a hard season of his life when he had nowhere to turn. Today Myron does the same for others in North Omaha.

Ron has released hundreds of people to be the people God has called them to be in unique ways. Ron is a multiplier. Bridge Church now has four locations throughout Omaha that have become hubs for hope. For many years, Ron has put his head down and served people in his community, raising up leaders and reminding them they have a mission from God Himself. You can read this developing story in Ron's book *Out of the Seats and into the Streets.*

No two stories look the same. Ron's life and ministry will look different from yours. Every person is unique. Every church is unique. Every community is unique. Obey the Father. Don't just copy others.

DISCUSS THIS

- What is most authentic about the ministry you lead?
- From the list of new creatives in this chapter, which areas have you failed to recognize and affirm? Make a list of people who come to mind when you read through this list.
- What causes do you or your ministry currently engage? What new causes can you or your ministry engage?
- What new processes can you develop for identifying the unique genius in others around you?

CHAPTER 5

GENIUS IS A PROCESS

Talent is not a thing; it's a process.[1]
—David Shenk

I'm convinced that about half of what separates
the successful entrepreneurs from the
nonsuccessful ones is pure perseverance.[2]
—Steve Jobs

There is nothing new under the sun.
—Ecclesiastes 1:9

I had no idea which direction I needed to run. I felt a gnaw-
ing pressure in my gut to make a decision soon. I had several
good options for the next step of my career. The only thing that
wouldn't work was staying where I was and doing more of what
I had been doing.

I decided to take off into the mountains for a twenty-four-
hour retreat to settle it. If I did my part of packing my car and
driving to a quiet place, surely God would deliver a quick answer
in the thin Rocky Mountain air. If I did the math right, I would

drive back to town with full confidence in my next step and share the decision with my wife in a perfect moment of clarity. But God laughed at my plans. As I was making final preparations, my stuff piled at the door, I received a call from another state with another opportunity. My confusion instantly turned into paralysis.

What started as a retreat in search of a convenient answer became an advance where I would duke it out with God. I drove away from the noise of the city, settled into a cabin, and waited. God wasn't checking a box like I had imagined. Instead, He ripped up my agenda.

So I went with Plan B: reading, napping, hiking, listening, waiting.

Still, I pressed God for an answer. *All I need to know is what I'm supposed to do, God. Then I can head down the mountain and start doing it.*

During those twenty-four hours God bypassed everything about my career and spoke to me instead about . . . me. "What should I do?" bent the knee to "Who am I?" As He began to reveal who He had made me to be, I wrote as fast as my hand could move. My journal transformed into a canvas for soul poetry. An obscure book transformed into a long-distance therapy session with an author who lives two thousand miles away.

Twenty-four hours later I had my answer. It didn't go as planned. God told me who I was—and who I wasn't. He spoke to me about my soul. My heart became the canvas, not a box to check. It wasn't neat and clean. There was still work to do.

After the deeply spiritual practice of fasting that day, I drove straight to a Wendy's and feasted on a few burgers and fries. Forgive me, Lord.

Then my wife and I prayed and enjoyed the evening together. And God promptly closed the final door I had been praying about.

Through the process of elimination, the answer was to stay and just keep going. I wanted a quick fix, but God wanted to teach me to trust, to labor, to stretch.

- We often seek God for an answer when He wants to teach us a process.
- We want a to-do list with boxes to check, but He wants to dive below the surface.
- We yearn for a calling or career that seems more adventurous, but God wants to reshape the topography of our souls.
- We want a microwaved faith, but God pulls out a Crock-Pot.
- We are preoccupied with who we wish we were, but God wants to remind us who He's wired us to be.

Following Jesus into the great unknown isn't a transactional moment; it's an adventurous process. Somehow it looks easy for others, but don't be fooled; it will take work. It will take wrestling. You might be sore afterward. Your soul might pull a hamstring. It's hard to stuff God into a box. It's never worked very well for me.

Genius doesn't emerge as we might imagine. Genius is given by God, but it is honed through process. It takes discipline to continue creating over an extended time. In his book *Divine Fury*, Darrin McMahon wrote, "Few ideas—even if ideas of genius— emerge from nothing, *ex nihilo*, without any precedents at all."[3] And Ecclesiastes reminds us "there is nothing new under the sun."

When I'm driving, sometimes I get a sudden idea. I have to pull over and write it down. When I'm in the shower I get a brilliant thought for an upcoming sermon. When I'm hiking on a beautiful Colorado day, I see a problem or a challenge in a unique way and think of a solution. Sometimes I see an image and get an idea for a painting or a logo. Inspiration can come in a flash, but creative works aren't completed without blood, sweat, and discipline. You can't write a book, start a company, or complete an album on a whim.

Inspiring moments are the exception to the rule of genius. We love the idea of overnight success from golfers on the PGA Tour to music prodigies to rookie baseball pitchers to get-rich-quick schemers. The more I get to know talented people in different fields, the more I have tried to understand their stories.

People don't get to genius overnight; it's a process. Writer David Shenk observed, "While moments of inspiration do exist, great work is, for the most part, painstaking."[4] There is hard work, practice, investment, and commitment behind the scenes of their lives. And that doesn't seem as glorious as the overnight success fairy tales we like to believe.

People are curious about writing. There are so many perceptions of how ideas get translated into pages. The most common reaction I get when talking to someone about writing is, "I could never write a book." And I respond, "You might be surprised. I would have said that a while back."

Perhaps you are reading this book thinking, *How does someone fill a whole book?* I used to ask that question, but today I wonder, *How do I hone that book down to fifty thousand words?* We have far more to say than can be written; the real challenge is in organizing our thoughts and taking the time to write them down.

Every Tuesday morning I crawl out of bed while it's still dark, and I write for three hours. I'm not naturally a morning person. I don't wake up with birds chirping and shutters flying open like they do in a Disney movie. That's not me. If that's you, you kind of drive me crazy, and I'm also jealous. I get up early out of discipline and slowly wake up with the help of the Holy Spirit and caffeine.

I sit at a table at a coffee shop as silent curmudgeon for three hours. The dead of winter can be brutal, as I write for nearly two hours in the dark. But I've never had complete writer's block during those hours. I've never lacked for a thought, a story, quotes to transcribe, or a Scripture passage that applies.

There are many ways to organize creativity. A prolific author told me to lock myself in a cabin for a few weeks and write. Eat. Sleep. Write. Get cabin fever. Take a walk. Write some more. Repeat. Creative processes vary, but I have yet to meet someone who regularly takes on huge creative tasks and doesn't have a process. One author describes herself as a creative mule, trudging and bumping along the creative process.[5] The long-term creative race favors the mule, not the stallion.

Misconceptions About Creativity

When I talk to leaders about their dreams, I hear a lot of talk about "someday." I am tired of that word. I realize it's not always time to put a dream into action, but there is a general sense of apathy connected to the word *someday*. It lulls people to sleep. Producing anything of value takes intention and sacrifice. Leadership guru John Maxwell noted: "Everything worthwhile is uphill. People have uphill hopes and downhill habits."[6]

The creative process doesn't seem natural. It often feels forced. It takes discipline. Writing a book is not what I thought it would be, not as easy, free-flowing, or effortless as I imagined. Musicians have told me the same thing about recording an album. But I have learned to work the process. I have learned to chain myself to a desk and become a mule.

I saw a poster recently that perfectly describes the creative process:

1. This is awesome.
2. This is tricky.
3. This is c**p.
4. I am c**p.
5. This might be okay.
6. This is awesome.

Don't be surprised when you fade toward a sinking discouragement about your work.

Don't be surprised when you feel dull and stale.

Don't be surprised when you feel like your church is headed in exactly the wrong direction.

Don't be surprised when creative processes don't feel like fun.

It turns out the creative process can be brutal, boring, vulnerable, and uninspiring at many points along the journey. But it's worth it.

Imagine if those around you with significant talent got serious about submitting themselves to the creative process. The results would be unstoppable. The majority of the creatives I meet believe highly in inspiration and moments of emotion, but they struggle to apply any kind of discipline. The absence of process and structure leaves creatives waiting for the rare moments of inspiration scarcely dotted among the busyness of life. Most pastors I know find themselves preparing last-minute sermons in isolation. That's not a recipe for continual creativity.

One of my friends takes creativity and processes very seriously. After launching into a new career and business idea, he said, "If you want God to do something new, you can't keep doing the same old thing." So he asked himself two questions every morning before work and every day after work for the first ninety days after starting his company:

What do I need to stop doing today?
What do I need to start doing today?

These are great questions! We often try to see new results or tap into some new kind of creativity without changing our process or inputs. You will have to live with the tension of this irony: *to produce more, you will have to learn to do less.* And saying no is the first step to saying yes.

The natural urge to finish a long creative work is to simply work longer hours, to stuff more and more inside the bag. We try to become more productive and sleep less. Stress levels rise and priorities get out of balance. Two cups of coffee turn into six. Sounds a lot like my college days minus the frequent naps. It might work in the short term, but it's not sustainable. I am so passionate about helping leaders find a process that I wrote a free e-book called *Seven Steps to Launching Your Big Idea.* You can get it at my website.

Another friend just finished recording an album that has taken him several years to complete. I was there to purchase his very first CD. (I'm sure it'll be worth millions someday.) He has made the shift from creating when he can find time to dedicating himself each week to a creative process. It's not easy for him to exercise this kind of discipline, but it's been a breakthrough for him. He views creating music as part of his vocation, not just a side project.

Our culture bows the knee to genius. From Steve Jobs and the Apple revolution to the superhero status of LeBron James and his tomahawk dunks, we love to honor people for their superhuman abilities and creativity. We also like to think they were just born with them. We see young people with extreme gifts and believe they were simply born prolific.

Depression sets in the moment we look at ourselves in the mirror and think *I am only . . .* or *I am not . . .* If we look below the surface we will discover it took a lot of hard work and practice for Steve Jobs to become Steve Jobs and for LeBron James to become LeBron James. A *lot* of hard work. David Shenk pointed out: "Many crucial changes take place over long periods of time. Physiologically, it's impossible to become great overnight."[7]

Final-Draft Excellence with First-Draft Effort

We live in a world that wants final-draft excellence with first-draft effort. Creativity needs time to roast slowly over divine coals. The process of genius will skin up your knees and leave you in tears. "We live under the great myth of the perfect first draft."[8] There's good news, though. There are things we have been accidentally proficient at our whole lives that we can't see. We are distracted by the trees and can't see the breadth of the forest. That's why we need others.

We've all known someone who thought they were a genius

and others didn't agree. If you think you're a rock star and no one else does, then you'll find yourself singing solo hits in your garage at the tender age of fifty. We need others to help spot our genius and remind us of our potential. I wonder which of Steve Jobs's teachers saw his unique spark or had to kick him out of class for causing trouble. I wonder which coach taught LeBron James to play defense or made him run laps for not hustling.

There's a balance to excellence. If you continue to push into an area, and it never seems to move others, perhaps you are not holding onto hope but delusion. The people we trust can hold a mirror up to us, but be careful not to stake your full claim to success on what someone tells you. In most cases, other people have a more accurate picture than we have of ourselves. They can often validate and highlight the areas in which we are really gifted. I'll explore this more when I talk about the power of teams to hone genius.

Wading through critique is one of the hardest, most humbling things you can do. Critique renders us creatively naked in a land where others are wearing three-piece suits and gala dresses. Try to receive critique readily. And when you stand on the other side of the equation, be sure to critique others honestly and gently. A friend once told me the challenge of pastoring for the long haul hinges on having a soft heart and thick skin. It's probably true for artists also. We need to be ready to receive feedback that isn't pretty while remaining sensitive enough to see how God is at work in that moment.

Before I was a pastor, a leader I deeply respected told me he didn't believe I was cut out for full-time ministry. This was extremely confusing and a bit shocking. I had just worked through my fears of being a pastor and was ready to commit to ministry in a local church. I valued his opinion deeply, so I wrestled with that comment and with God. *Is he seeing something I'm not seeing?* Ultimately, God used that comment to bring me closer to Him and even clarify my vocational calling.

God often clarifies our call through struggle, experimentation, and failure. Even the most prolific geniuses didn't start by innovating but by practicing. For six years Wolfgang Mozart played almost nothing that was original. But after ten years of experimentation and practice, Mozart developed his own style and Symphony No. 29 in A major emerged. (A consensus of music historians believe this was his first great work.[9]) Be careful labeling others as a prodigy and yourself as a late bloomer.

Believing others are born superhuman relieves us of any expectation on ourselves. It can be a convenient way to excuse ourselves from working hard.[10]

So why should the creative process matter so much to followers of Jesus? Following are three reasons.

Stewardship

We are to be stewards of what God gives us. We aren't the makers, but we are the re-makers. We aren't creators, but we are the re-creators. The apostle Paul reminds us: *"This is how one should regard us, as servants of Christ and stewards of the mysteries of God. Moreover, it is required of stewards that they be found faithful"* (1 Cor. 4:1–2). This is a serious call to apply the gifts and abilities God has given us to His kingdom work.

Envy

Genius improperly applied leads us to envy. We often believe others were created brilliant while we were created mediocre. We compare their area of expertise to our areas of weakness. We fail to understand how they have worked hard to practice, apply themselves, and take risks to continue to create. Envy and jealousy snuff out gratitude, joy, and creativity. "Genius envy" is a sure path to losing your creativity and being ungrateful for what God has given you. Envy blocks faithfulness.

Expectations

Our expectations are often skewed. We expect to start an idea, a process, or a craft and immediately excel. As church leaders, we often expect to experience the same results we see in others as they lead ministries, teach, build teams, and engage the lost around them. We expect to see these same results for ourselves, and the pressure rises. Our fear of failure drives us to immediately seek greatness instead of seeking faithfulness.

In my book *Staying Is the New Going*, I talk about a much-needed paradigm shift in our culture from seeking impact to seeking faithful presence. If you aim at impact, you will likely be disappointed, but if you aim at faithful presence, you often experience impact. The hunger for impact is natural, but it drives us to unspiritual places. It's a longing that will never be satisfied. Today you'll want one thousand followers, but tomorrow you'll want five thousand more. The hunger for impact in American culture is nothing short of idolatry. We crave significance so much we are tempted to do anything to get it. It's never enough. These are misplaced desires.

The *S* Word

The word *structure* is a dirty word to me. It might as well have only four letters. Just the other day another one of my brilliant ideas was hijacked by the suggestion I should give it more structure and flesh out bullet points, directives, and measureables. I face this discouraging feeling nearly every week, but I have learned to see the good in it. These steps will often make my idea or process better.

I used to think structure was the enemy of creativity, but now I know it's crucial to the creative process. We need structure or our lives will fall apart. Andy Crouch, author of *Culture Making*, observed, "Creativity cannot exist without order."[11] Boundaries give us the space to create and the health to keep creating. Most of the people I coach are simply looking for healthy processes to continue unleashing their creativity.

When people within the church come to me with an idea, I usually need to give them structure. Every church leader hears some crazy ideas. Most of these ideas are really good and simply need some honing. Some of them are downright crazy. Part of our role as saint equippers (Eph. 4:11–12) is to help others put meat on the creative bones of those around us. People need guidelines and a little bit of guidance on how to proceed.

You Can't Afford Not to Sabbath

Rest has been demonized in our culture. People avoid it like the plague. It makes us appear weak, but nothing could be further from the truth. The Almighty modeled this great gift to us after He had finished His great masterpiece:

God had finished his work.

On the seventh day

    he rested from all his work.

God blessed the seventh day.

    He made it a Holy Day

Because on that day he rested from his work,

    all the creating God had done.

—Genesis 2:2–3 THE MESSAGE

Sabbath is one of the greatest boundaries you can ever set. It's also a gift. Sabbath is the energy reset button God gave us. Intentional rest opens the space for more creativity. Sabbath is a risk you can't afford to pass up. To take a break from creating and producing feels like a loss in the moment, but it always seems to come around to backfill that hole.

A friend is currently working on her dissertation. She is in the gut of it, pushing hard to finish. She commented to me that she was taking a break for the day, a Sabbath away from her paper, and trusting God would help her keep pushing. That was a good word. Sabbath lets the ground that has been producing lay fallow and gives the soil of our hearts, minds, and souls time to produce again.

If you don't take breaks from creating what you love, you will head toward burnout. At first you might think you can't afford to take a Sabbath, but eventually you will realize you can't afford not to.

Three Key Ingredients to the Creative Process

Affirmation

We are relational beings. The best and worst of what comes out in us has an impact on others. The best things in us can't fully emerge until they are called out by others. Talents, abilities, and creativity are confirmed in community. I know people who are chasing "someday" in areas in which they are not particularly gifted. There is a fine balance of honing our weaknesses and putting our best effort toward what we are uniquely gifted in.

All our voices sound like recording artists' when we are singing alone in the shower. God has wired us as communal beings who must call others into greater impact. The image of God is better reflected than ingested. Proverbs 27:17 reminds us *"iron sharpens iron, and one man sharpens another."* This is often used as an accountability verse, but this sharpening can also apply to affirming and validating the work of God in one another. We need to learn to speak confidently about where others excel.

Focused Work

The term *hard work* falls short when referring to the creative process. Malcolm Gladwell's ten-thousand-hour rule is more like it.[12] In his book *Outliers*, Gladwell recounted the thousands of hours the Beatles played to a revolving door of listeners in a pub in Hamburg. As they were playing together they found themselves. The world-famous Beatles did not become the Beatles we know the moment they met; they became the Beatles one chord at a time, one song at a time, one hour at a time. Their performances were also their practices.

We learn by doing. Practice isn't something we do before we perform, it is something we are always doing. Practice sharpens the edge of the blade we have been given.

Boundaries

People all around you are heading toward burnout. Don't be fooled by caffeinated drinks and busy schedules. Most people are barely surviving the frantic action and the humdrum boredom of life. We must learn boundaries.[13] When people get serious about practicing and guarding the Sabbath, creativity has space to flow more freely. Fruitfulness sprouts from boundaries. Don't have any fresh ideas? Go to bed. Don't feel any innovative solutions to your stuckness? Take a day at the park away from work.

Jesus retreated from the demands of ministry and leadership. When we rest, God works. When we pause, He can fill our empty glass back up. Jesus took care of Himself so He could keep taking care of others. Self-care is different from self-absorption. Parker Palmer noted, "Self-care is never a selfish act—it is simply good stewardship of the only gift I have, the gift I was put on earth to offer to others."[14] We can't afford to avoid boundaries and limits.

We have genius. We also have limits. Posters hang in local elementary schools telling us that we can be anyone we want to be. Not true. I took a few years of algebra, and I only understood it well enough to pass a few tests; I will never be an accountant or a financial analyst. There are things I want to do and I cannot. There are also things I am gifted to do that I am working hard to hone.

Stewardship will put you on a steady diet of humble pie. When I refer to limits, I am not referring to the limitations others force on you as a means of oppression. That is ungodly. Limits are natural. We were all born with them, and we must come to terms with them. Parker Palmer observed, "Each of us arrives here with a nature, which means both limits and potentials."[15] Anyone who has ever written a book will tell you about the gift of an editor. This book would be much longer and make very little logical sense without my editor.

Discover Your Story to Tell

A leader entered my city with a burning heart to use his gifts to plant a church and have a significant impact on the whole city.

I work with church planters, and I love their never-say-die attitude and caffeinated personalities. But I have learned to ask some deep heart-level questions to have them look beyond their passion and drive.

Several times I suggested this leader connect with other ministry leaders and pastors who were already doing great work in the city. There were several groups that welcomed him with open arms. Connecting leaders for collaboration is a huge value to me. We all need a "freaks like me" club where we are reminded we are completely normal yet completely unique. God uses these groups to work down the spectrum of *friendship >> partnership >> collaboration* that I talked about earlier in the book.

But this dude was so busy "getting ministry done" and starting new things that he was not excited to join in the things that were already going on.

Within a few months, he perceived no one was taking him seriously or listening to his ideas. I explained the rule of longevity—*consistency yields credibility*—but he wasn't getting it.

One day we met, and God seemed to have knocked some of the hard edges off him. He described a conversation with an older sage in his life. He shared similar thoughts about his longing for influence in our city with him. The man listened and said: "You don't have a story to tell yet. Find your story, and then you can influence others." He was floored. The audacity! He laughed because he knew it was true.

Seek to be a servant and a steward, and God often adds

influence when He believes we are ready. Kevin Palau wisely noted, "As leaders, we need to seek service, not influence."[16] We need to trade our obsession with influence for a posture of faithful presence. God is authoring our stories, and we are just characters playing our part.

DISCUSS THIS

- What do you need to *stop* doing in order to steward your creativity?
- What do you need to *start* doing in order to steward your creativity?
- What creative processes do you regularly practice? How effective are they?
- What processes do you have to give and receive feedback? How can they become more effective?
- Where are you chasing impact?
- How do you regularly practice Sabbath? How can you grow in this?
- What boundaries have helped you to continually create? What boundaries do you need to add to your process?

CHAPTER 6

GENIUS GONE WRONG

One needs only to do the math to see
the high cost of destructive genius.[1]
—Liz Wiseman

Most people never get the opportunity to be
meaningfully involved in the working of the system.
—Max De Pree

The church must move from the destructively
familiar to the creatively strange.[2]
—Rowan Williams

Something had gone very wrong. I woke up incredibly overwhelmed. All I could think about were the challenges that
lay ahead of me the next few weeks. Details. Administration.
Complications. Scheduling. Complaints. All things I struggle
with, but all of which have become necessary evils to get to the
good of equipping leaders for mission.

It wasn't supposed to be this way. My wife and I were away for
a few days, celebrating our anniversary under the snowcapped

Colorado peaks. Nice dinners, romance, and the mountains are incredible gifts, but my wife and I were most excited to sleep late two days in a row. I know, our marriage sounds ablaze with passion. These few days were supposed to be a chance to get away from the mess of life, the chaos of schedules in a family of six, and a chance to explore the back roads of my beautiful state. There were supposed to be no worries during these few days. As it turned out, worry travels pretty well.

I looked at my wife, fast asleep and enjoying the pillow as I should've been. I tossed and turned a bit before finally deciding to take advantage of the bad hotel coffee and a predictable continental breakfast. This wasn't what I had planned. I might as well have stayed home and rolled over with a coughing child or two in my bed.

Perhaps you can identify. Everything was perfect, but something snuck up and stole the joy away. It is easy to write this off as part of the curse or the stress of a life that is strangely normal. But I think we need to look a bit deeper. It wasn't that I was worrying that morning; it was more about what I was tossing and turning and worrying about.

I could have been stressed about a number of things that morning. I had several deadlines ahead of me for both speaking events and writing projects. People were asking me if I was stressed about these deadlines, and the honest truth was that I wasn't.

I was worrying about all the details behind these deadlines and wondering how they were going to come together. To someone else, those details might seem like child's play. But I would rather talk to a stadium of ten thousand people on a whim or be down to the wire on a hard writing deadline than have to schedule all that I was in charge of doing. All these details were overwhelming me.

I rarely wake up stressed about my areas of gifting. Stress, however, almost always bites me in my areas of weakness. The reality is that I was trying to lead outside of my strengths, and all that administrative work was buckling down on me.

That morning was a painful watershed moment. I came to the end of myself and began to ask for help in certain areas. I expressed to my team how I couldn't continue carry this administrative load.

When we live primarily out of our weaknesses, we find ourselves in moments, even seasons of paralysis. When we live in our strengths, we might find ourselves pushed to our creative limits—but loving it. There is a weight to both, but we will pay a never-ending price for living in our weaknesses instead of our genius.

I'm not saying you are perfectly wired for everything you do. We all have responsibilities we wish weren't on our plate. There is toil on this earth. My email in-box is a constantly nipping at my heels. If I've avoided an email from you, chances are it was just a mistake on my end.

Events take massive amounts of administration that come close to drawing all the life out of me before the event even begins. But there are necessary evils in your vocation. There are things you are not wired to do but God tells you to do them anyway. There are things in your job, family, and friendships you will need to carry that you aren't wired to carry long term. Those things have their place, but your area of genius should be filling up most of your creative time and energy.

A friend became aware of all the time he had wasted instead of focusing on his genius. After moving to a new city, his first commitment to settle down was to regularly apply himself to his craft. He committed to practicing what he was most gifted at with most of his energy. Not surprisingly, he experienced a breakthrough. He completed creative projects he had left in the balance for five years.

When most people think about genius gone wrong, they might reference horrific tyranny in human history. Most times, genius gone wrong involves subtle killers sneaking into our camp. I'm talking about fear, pride, and comparison. These killers can leave us thinking we haven't been invited to the creative party but everyone else in the class got the invite.

Silent Genius Assassins

Let's dig into these silent genius assassins: fear, pride, and comparison.

Fear

We all feel it. At some level it's healthy. Those who claim they feel no fear in a risk are either lying or crazy. Maybe both. Fear is a marker of reality, not a limiter of destiny. If we let fear grip us, our congregations, and our teams, we unconsciously snuff out faith. Faith dares to take a risk and leans on the Father to overcome the fear factor. Unchecked fear causes us to recoil, hide, act calmly on the outside while we are petrified within. We all feel fear. Admit it. Pray through it. Measure the measly depths of your fear against the breadth of the gospel and watch your heart take courage.

Pride

Pride tells us we don't need to work hard. We deserve it. We can take it easy. I sit with Christian leaders at the edge of risk a lot. Perhaps they are starting a ministry, a church, a business, or a creative process. A leader recently asked to meet with me so he could share a big idea. I didn't know him, but he was from several states away, so I changed my schedule to accommodate him.

He did not ask one question the whole time we talked. He only waxed eloquent, talking about how others had gotten it wrong, but he had the solution. What he didn't know was I had a list of three leaders who could have been great ministry partners for him. I didn't give him the list. He never asked. Pride causes us to talk down about others who don't agree with us or have a different focus. Pride kills both creativity and collaboration.

Comparison

The fastest way to bring a creative process to a screeching halt is to compare yourself to others. Only moments after reveling in the joy of something you've accomplished, your heart sinks because someone else received more posts, more funding, more hits, more tweets, more recognition, more stage time, or more attention than you. Comparison is death to dreaming and poison to your creativity.

A moment of comparison leaves you open to Satan's whispers: *You don't have what it takes . . . You aren't creative . . . special . . . significant.* I find that when I am tired, I am particularly susceptible to these lies. When you get tired, cease producing and let God refill what has been poured out. Sometimes going to bed is the most spiritual thing you can do. Recognize when it's time to steer clear of social media, which is sure to remind you of how others excel and you are below the bar.

Comparison is probably the biggest genius assassin of them all. I distinctly remember a time when comparison left me feeling discouraged. I was thrilled to be welcomed into a particular gathering. I was just dipping my toe into conversations about planting churches, and I had been invited to spend a few days with some seasoned practitioners in this field. I looked around the room, fully aware I was the youngest and most inexperienced. I took notes during every session, shutting my mouth because I didn't feel like I had anything to offer. I was honored to be in the room but discouraged about the leader I wasn't and the leaders *they* were. I thought, *I don't belong here. Why did I get on a plane for this?* Comparing IQs and experiences caused me to believe a false narrative that day.

Comparison leads to discouragement. The genius we see in others can remind us of our lack of talent, skills, and experience. This leads us straight to insecurity. It can also narrowly define genius when we don't fit in a particular box. We are obsessed with comparison in our culture, and it's crippling the church today. We wonder why another leader gets to experience so much fruit. When things are a bit stale at our church, we look for ideas that are working at other churches. When we believe God is moving at the church across the street, we are tempted to believe our diminishing numbers confirm God's diminishing blessing on us.

There is something encouraging yet discouraging about seeing others excel in a skill. We think: *They are the geniuses. They are innovative, amazing communicators, and intensely creative.* We all slip into this destructive thinking sometimes. Instead of being encouraged by a conference or book, we wonder why we're not speaking onstage or why we weren't asked to write a book. (Don't act like you haven't thought that. You're human.) When we see others do amazing things, we think, *These extraordinary performers cannot possibly belong to the same species as me.*[3] We are left to conclude God has withheld something from us that He should have given.

Comparison leads to individualism. When we talk about the genius God has buried in each person, we need to be careful not to worship at the altar of individualism. Every individual, every team, and every church is unique. Will Mancini has pointed out: "Local churches are unmistakably unique and incomparably different. God doesn't mass produce his church."⁴

Yes, we are all unique, but we are all humans created in the deep creative well of the Father. Individualism is different from uniqueness. Individualism focuses on why we are different from everyone else. It leads to a striving to stand out, perform, and succeed as an individual. It can yield loneliness and separate us from others. Uniqueness is a focus on how God has fashioned each person creatively. The focus here is not on how we're different, but on how God celebrates creativity as part of the created order. It's a reminder that we possess God-given, others-directed gifts, and we simply can't avoid being unique. Take comfort: you are completely normal and completely unique at the same time.

On my worst days, when I'm a mess, I need to know I'm not alone. Struggling and wrestling are part of the human experience. I also need to know I'm unique, that my fingerprint is the only one like it in the world, and my makeup is not a copy of someone else's. Creation echoes with uniqueness and normality, and so do we. Be aware of fear, pride, and comparison that Satan casts out to lure and hook you.

Three Idols in Our Culture

We live in strange days. Cultural exegesis is a necessary skill to navigate the waters of our culture and have an impact within our community. The following three things often transform from their rightful role in life into idols to which we bow a knee.

- Celebrity: We long to be known, to be recognized. This longing leaks out through our obsession with stalking celebrities. The paparazzi snap pictures of Hollywood stars on dates, in traffic, and going to yoga class. Who really cares! Well, for some reason, we all seem to care. Our culture is full of people who are famous for being famous. We are drawn to celebrity and have a bad habit of worshiping it.
- Event: We long for a big event, the completion of a dream. The event is not bad in and of itself, but it can become an obsession. Events feel more validating than processes. It's easy to equate fruit and obedience with the sense of fulfillment we experience during events. Left unchecked, this desire will liken our churches to calendars full of events instead of people full of redemptive stories. Our longing for the big event is simply a misplaced longing for *the* big event we will one day experience in heaven.
- Start-up: We long to start something of meaning. Our culture values self-built leaders who create something from scratch and pull themselves up by their bootstraps. Entrepreneurs become our heroes. Kingdom work, however, isn't about starting something but about joining God in His work.

Ironically all three of these longings are expressed in the desire to plant a church. Somewhere in the birth of every new church is the question, How can we do this better than it's been done before? Church planters often get tangled in these three snares of celebrity, event, and start-up. A desire to honor God through the presence, mission, and formation of a local community of faith often becomes an obsession. These are misplaced longings that will render you always stressed and never satisfied.

Where Spiritual Gift Assessments Went Wrong

We talk a lot about spiritual gifts. And rightly so. They give a lot of direction for the variety of gifts God has given to His church. Over the past few decades spiritual gift assessments have become wildly popular. I have led some of these assessments, and they have been very helpful for people to discover their wiring and ministry niche. But we must be careful of spiritual gifts assessments going wrong in a few ways.

Hierarchies of Greater and Lesser Gifts

Every time I get ready to lead a group of people into a spiritual gifts assessment, it is met with fear. People share how they always come up with the lesser gifts on their assessment. They are left feeling like the greater gifts are teaching and leadership, because our culture and churches seem to esteem these more. People are left feeling that hospitality, serving, mercy, and administration are chump change that God doesn't value because North American churches don't seem to value them. Ouch!

Those folks leave assessments discouraged instead of encouraged. Validating certain gifts can also lead to a false sense of gifting or a deep desire to be gifted a certain way. This leads to a lack of desire to use the gifts God has given us and the feeling of a lesser ministry if we are stuck with "the lesser gifts."

Spiritual Gifts Are More About Us than How We Can Serve Others

Uncovering our spiritual gifts is not the end but a means to joining God's mission of bringing His message to the world. They are a starting place, but we are not limited to *only* serving God in those ways. It's impossible to limit every way we can bless the world—the list is endless. The ways God can use each person are as unique as a snowflake and a fingerprint.

Spiritual gifts can accidentally become a title we bear on the outside. Personality assessments can do the same. We might label ourselves as an activator because a StrengthsFinder told us we are an ENTJ because Myers and Briggs labeled us as such. We might conveniently remind others we are introverts when we want them to leave our homes so we can reconnect with our old friend Netflix. We might say we are a golden retriever because we are a helpful companion. We are not a summation of our gifts and personality assessments; we are God's children with souls, beating hearts and unique genius.

Gifts Are Only Organized As Ways to Serve the Church Body

Most courses and assessments on spiritual gifts only suggest ways to serve the church. People believe the gift of hospitality limits them to hosting small groups, brewing coffee at a church café, or making the best seven-layer Jell-O at a potluck. Most people are bored, even disappointed by these realizations.

What if, instead, we let people dream of ways they could serve coworkers, local nonprofits, or their neighbors with their hospitality? Those with mercy gifts might not have a counseling degree, but they might want to volunteer at a hospital or help immigrants gain access to basic needs. People want the freedom to dream about becoming community advocates and kingdom ambassadors in the name of Jesus.

Guided by Genius, Rooted in Love

Our gifts allow us to take flight but love tethers us to others. Love is essential to practicing redemptive creativity and to living well. Writer and professor James K. A. Smith noted: "If you are passionate about seeking justice, renewing culture, and taking up your vocation to unfurl all of creation's potential, you need to invest in the formation of your imagination. You need to curate your heart. You need to worship well. Because you are what you love."[5] We are tethered to God's love, and that redemptive story teaches us to live well within our story.

One of the greatest temptations about using our creativity is to seek the power that comes through influence. We are to choose love instead. The late Henri Nouwen pointed out this danger: "The long painful history of the church is a history of people ever and again tempted to choose power over love, control over the cross, being a leader over being led."[6] God gives us creativity so we might clearly express our love to Him and to the world around us.

It is love that will endear the people of Jesus to our world. It is winsome. People are thirsting for something greater than money and consumption. We are exiting an age of production into an age of meaning. Business thinker Seth Godin explained, "Factories created productivity, and productivity produced profits."[7] Societal shifts, the changing needs of the workforce, and new technology are causing our culture to spin faster than ever. Creatives, artists, designers, consultants, activists, makers, and foodies seem to be inventing new job descriptions every week, ones that didn't exist a decade ago. Activism is skyrocketing. People are advocating for every cause imaginable. Nearly everyone I meet, no matter how old, is preoccupied with changing the world. Humans are hounds sniffing for meaning.

Here's the good news: The potential to unleash the creativity of God's people and tangibly bless the world has never been greater. But the church is trying to play catch-up. We need a grid for clearly and simply expanding our view of what joining God's mission should look like, feel like, and taste like in this changing world. We need to recover a creative imagination.

A handful of friends are intently using their creativity as a reflective platform for Jesus. One is a third-wave barista and coffee educator, sharing the intricacies of the economy it creates and the proper ways of preparing it. Another is a visual storyteller who unearths beautiful storylines of how the mission of their organization is coming to life. Another works for a growing and influential company and views himself as a cultural director charged with shaping the ethos of the staff. Another designs faith-based apps. Another is a principal living out his faith to students, teachers, and parents. There is no limit to how God's people can use their creativity for the sake of the world.

My friends have credibility in spaces where I don't. And the door is open for God's people to connect and influence nearly every cultural crevice in nearly every vocation. Limitations are lifting and opportunities are starting to float to the surface, but there is still a big gap.

The key to ministry in the twenty-first century will be discovering, unlocking, and releasing people to live out their

God-given abilities on different stages. This will primarily happen beyond the walls of the church where others have influence.

Church leaders, we simply must take seriously our role as saint equippers. Most church leaders feel the urgency of this moment. We can spend our time fixated on those who are leaving the church or we can expend serious energy on those who are still sitting in the pews ready to do something fresh.

In his book *The Artisan Soul,* Erwin McManus asked questions about the collision of anthropology and theology. His thesis is that we have some wrong assumptions and some critical questions to answer. Here's the real question, "Is every human inherently creative?"[8] I believe the answer is a resounding *yes!* That's why I simply had to write this book.

We Are Doulas

Everyone seems to have contentious opinions about pregnancy and childbirth. Eat this. Don't eat that. Give birth at home. Give birth in a hospital. An epidural is a gift from God Himself. Natural childbirth is for the pure in heart. Whatever your view about these things, try not to punch someone in the jaw when they share a differing view.

Doulas are becoming increasingly more common in the birthing process. It took me a while to understand what a doula is. The dictionary defines it as "a woman experienced in childbirth who provides advice, information, emotional support, and physical comfort to a mother before, during, and just after childbirth."[9] Doulas don't actually deliver babies like an ob-gyn or a nurse.

The Greek word *doulas* means "servant." And Christian

leaders should function more like doulas. (Michael Frost and Christianna Rice discuss this at length in their book *To Alter the World.*) We can equip, coach, support, inform, and comfort others. Doulas come alongside pregnant moms to serve. Doulas cannot control conception or delivery, but they coach and help where they can. We are servants and stewards of God's work.

This has been a pretty negative chapter. And I hope this gets it out of the way so we can wade into the warm waters of hope. I simply couldn't avoid talking about the snags and snares Satan wants us to believe to hold us back from having an impact outside the church family.

DISCUSS THIS

- What fears get in the way of your creativity?
- In which areas have you been comparing yourself to others? What has the result been?
- How does pride get in the way of your creativity?
- What gifts have been affirmed as *greater gifts* in your ministry context? *Lesser gifts?*

CHAPTER 7

THE CHURCH AS
GENIUS FACTORY

The real test of leadership and influence is when we're
willing to stand behind others and let them shine.[1]
—Jenni Catron

Mistakes aren't a necessary evil. They
aren't evil at all. They are an inevitable
consequence of doing something new.[2]
—Ed Catmull

Never doubt that a small group of committed
people can change the world; indeed,
it's the only thing that ever has.
—Margaret Mead

What does your church produce? I know the church isn't a
factory in the sense of producing tangible goods at a
market price. As hard as we might try, we can't quantify transformation or the price of a soul. But every church produces

something. Some churches produce discontent, some missionaries, some excellence, some world changers, some frustration, and some disciples. But we all must produce faith in our people. The church can be a pseudo-functional family amidst a world of dysfunctional families. The church can be a family continually asking, "How will you leverage this one life you've been given for the glory of God?" Church leadership must model this by giving our best time to equipping and empowering the people who want to take risks to leverage their lives. Faith and obedience sit at the knife's edge of failure. If spending time developing people weren't a risk, it wouldn't require faith.

There's a lot at stake here. Church leaders are diverse as cities. All those Paul refers to in Ephesians 4:11–12 exist to equip the saints for ministry. We need to put our best energy into being saint equippers. I believe God gives us a lot of leeway on how to do this, but He puts a clear emphasis on the need to do this. When we identify and hone others' genius, we literally get to partner with them to watch their soul come alive. Tom Paterson observed, "Show me a person who doesn't know his talents, or hasn't developed them for service to others, and I will show you a person who has little sense of purpose, meaning, motivation and value."[3] The seeds of meaningful service yield a crop of meaning.

We should have this culture in our churches. Church leadership champion Will Mancini noted, "Culture is the combined effect of the interacting values, thoughts, attitudes and actions that define the life of your church."[4] Those should all collide in our desire to develop God's people, the church. The word should get out that the church is a group of people who recognize and leverage their gifts.

Take time to analyze your church. Is it a priority of the church leadership to recognize genius and equip the congregation to do ministry? Often we get stuck on the things churches should *provide* (knowledge of God's Word, an environment to connect with others, discipleship opportunities) and forget about creating a culture where genius is *discovered, affirmed,* and *unleashed.*

We've oversold the accumulation of knowledge and undersold learning through relationships and experiences. I grew up just minutes from a beautiful Ivy League university. I didn't have the grades to get in, nor did I want to. As a kid I thought college was all about cheering for your school at the football game and carrying your friends out of the stadium when they were beyond drunk. These are some of my early memories. You might assume all Ivy League universities are top notch because they have the smartest professors who all have superior knowledge. To many, Harvard is the apex of formal education. A prominent humanitarian said, "The best thing Harvard has to offer is the out-of-school, out-of-class education . . . the resources, mentors, opportunities, friends."[5]

Most churches have a lot of relational resources to offer. The focus of leadership development in our churches should far exceed our focus on excellence. We need to be willing to lower our bar of excellence so we can raise the bar of leadership development. Every church should seek to become a genius pipeline and deployment center.

Celebrating Creativity

In chapter 1, I mentioned the global phenomenon of TED events. One of their stages could feature any idea in our solar system or a solar system near us. It could feature a PhD, a soccer coach, a physicist, a student, an artist, a teacher, a dropout, a graphic designer, a musician, a pastor, or any number of professions. This has hit a nerve. I am deeply inspired and slightly saddened when I watch TED talks. I wish the church could celebrate people and their work like TED does. The church needs to celebrate creativity and innovation more than any other organization on earth while still adhering to the age-old life and teachings of Jesus.

Creativity is no longer relegated to professionals in creative careers. Many fields are undergoing a shift away from professionals to everyday creatives. Take the spike in photography for example. World-renowned photographer Chase Jarvis has noted this shift. In the age of smartphone photography, he has observed and embraced the shift away from the age of professional photography to the age of accessible photography. The quality and quantity of great photos has skyrocketed. Chase said, "The best camera is the one you have on you."[6]

Just like Chase, we need to resist the impulse to think that seasoned professionals are better than passionate amateurs. Instead, we need to stop looking at the tools we haven't been given and start utilizing the ones we have. Perhaps the best gifts are the ones we have in us, and the leaders with the most potential are the ones who are already under our noses.

Environments Matter

Whenever people walk into a new environment, they smell, taste, feel, hear, and see things immediately. But over time we accidentally become immune to these things. We lose our fresh eyes to see the good, bad, ugly, and confusing things about the environments we help to create. An environment is a reflection of the collective heart of those who have shaped it. When I was growing up, my parents—especially my mom—shaped an environment of care and love around our dining room table. This instilled a passion in me to welcome people to our home, our lives, and our table. Environments matter in our homes, businesses, churches, relationships, and neighborhoods.

Jesus always created environments of connection. In His presence outsiders felt welcome, hard-hearted souls felt challenged, the unlovely felt loved, and the needy felt full. Jesus was the genius environment creator. Environments mattered to Jesus, and they should matter to us.

Collective Environments Matter

Churches are starting to think more about environments today. Once people feel welcome in a church family, will they feel challenged, distracted, cared for, supported, affirmed, or unleashed? We need to think more about whether our environments are inviting people into growth, discipleship, and risk. Discipleship is a beautiful and rugged journey into living like Jesus. *Are we expressing both the beauty and struggle of following Jesus?* The disciples got to experience miracles and became the core team that started a movement. Many of them were persecuted and killed for it. Young leaders tell me they want to be like Paul. So I ask them if they are excited about doing some prison time.

Personal Environments Matter

The personal environments we shape matter as well. The home is not a refuge *from* ministry but a hub *for* ministry.[7] Yes, we need to have boundaries for our families, but ministry should be pouring out of our homes and into our neighborhoods. Your life should be open enough that people can walk into it when they are hungry for Jesus. My dad has always held influential positions, which keeps his plate full, but somehow he is almost always available whenever my brother or I call. He has created space in his life where people know they are the main thing, not an interruption.

Perhaps the greatest turnoff to the personal environment we have created around us is busyness. I know a leader who is always stressed and overwhelmed. I am not going to ask him to do more or process an idea when I sense he's already overloaded. I have functioned like this for weeks or seasons of my life and ministry. It's a battle I am committed to keep fighting. That's not the environment I want to invite others into.

Several years ago, I realized I was on what ministry leaders refer to as the ministry "treadmill." We can crank up the dial and run faster, and we may experience some short-term wins, but we are also exhausting ourselves. Most pastors in America are on the ministry treadmill. Most feel exhausted and ineffective. There are scores of books on this subject, but I think it could most easily be narrowed down to a lack of rhythm and rest that results in a deformed me-centric theology.

Since my ministry treadmill season, I committed to a Sabbath every week and to never fill my weekly schedule more than 80 percent full. This leaves space to respond to God, to be open to meet with people who want to talk, and to adjust to the interruptions that inevitably arise. This has allowed me to maintain a priority for people. We need to maintain accessibility without promising continual availability.

Occasionally a big event comes up, and I am in a focused (sometimes frantic) mode to accomplish everything. Recently I had one of those weeks, and I was tempted to say no to things I am committed to do every week. I started to rationalize. I told myself others would understand. I wrestled. I was tempted to sacrifice the important for the urgent. I decided to stick with the original plan, and I was glad I had kept my priorities straight. Details will always get done, but we need to keep battling to keep our focus on people.

When I try to focus on my work around my kids, I get frustrated. They "bother" me by poking me or yelling at a sibling. Sometimes I'm so focused on so-called "important things" on my laptop that I don't want my youngest daughter to snuggle up in my lap. One time my son wanted to talk, and I told him: "Daddy needs to be left alone. He is reading the Bible." That'll preach as the next example of how not to be a terrible dad. I've learned that my living room is the worst place to try to get work done.

The consistency of your creativity depends on the environment you create. Find the right spaces and frames of mind for what you are hoping to accomplish. Some leaders work well in an office, some in a coffee shop, and some at home.

Pastor and author Mark Batterson developed an equation: *Change of Pace + Change of Place = Change of Perspective.*[8] This is incredibly helpful. Find the space that gives you a reprieve from your everyday perspective. Turn your phone to airplane mode and disable the wireless on your computer.

Some of the best writing advice I ever received was to find a place that lights you up, get a hot beverage you enjoy, and let the writing flow.

Artist Makoto Fujimura, in his amazing mixture of words and images in his book *Refractions,* challenges readers to designate a space where they can commit to regularly creating something. Find the environment and timeframe where you can be creative and commit to regularly creating. You can grab my free e-book *7 Steps to Launching Your Big Idea* at my site for help defining your creative process.

Here are some questions to evaluate the environment you create:

- What do people sense when they first meet you?
- Do you celebrate the diversity and quirkiness of others? If so, how?
- What spaces and times are you most creative? Are you consistently committed to that time and space for creativity?
- Is your home, table, or couch a welcoming place? Why or why not?
- How often do you eat with the people you want to include in your life?
- Do you and your family have a culture of invitation into your life? Why or why not?
- Have the boundaries you have created helped make you more or less effective at loving others?
- How often are you giving your attention to those who don't yet know Jesus?

Five Responses to Culture

How we choose to respond to culture is a big deal. Perhaps people sometime in the past grew up in a black-and-white world where the differences between right and wrong were easy to spot in the eyes of the culture. Today, we live in a gray world where we, as followers of Jesus, must wrestle with our response to our host culture hourly, sifting for discernment. In his must-read book *Culture Making*, Andy Crouch gives five ways we can interact with our culture: condemn, critique, copy, consume, or create.[9]

Condemn Culture

Fear is the biggest reason Christians condemn culture. Clearly we need discernment as there are things lurking in our broken world that can take us down. Much of the underbelly of the holiness movement and fundamentalist tradition involved avoidance of possible sinful environments. It became defined by what *it* wasn't instead of what *it* was.[10] Condemning culture creates a fearful, negative environment. Instead of a positive message of pursuing holiness in Christ, this became a negative message: the world is bad, stay away.

Critique Culture

In an effort to engage culture, often the church is simply critiquing it. It is easy to speak against what we don't understand. Instead, we can acknowledge art and creation as a heart cry. There is truth buried there, and we find longings of a world that is not whole. We can't afford to miss these opportunities to engage the hearts of artists, activists, or entrepreneurs. Within our world, a carefully tuned ear will hear cries for the "good life."[11]

Copy Culture

We have to go beyond imitation. The goal is not to find a Christian version of everything in culture, from branding to music to conferences. Walk through a Christian bookstore, and you'll find myriad products redressing the cultural mannequin from Minecraft Bibles to Christian T-shirts (don't get me started on these). I call these things "Jesus junk." They don't show the image of the Creator; they show a cheap, cheesy counterfeit of culture. Artists are not drawn to this; they are repulsed by it.

Consume Culture

Today, most Christians don't avoid movies—as they were once told to do—or critique them carefully for dangers.[12] We have been inoculated to them. We are in danger of simply consuming them, immersing in their thrills without seeing their vices. Simple consumption is perhaps the most subtly dangerous of all the ways of relating to culture.

In the months following the Oscars my wife and I watch all the Oscar nominated films and discuss the messages below the storylines. We can't simply take our biblical lenses off and ingest culture without asking deeper questions about it. We need to teach others the process of asking discerning questions about mass media.

Create or Cultivate Culture

We are built to cultivate things, people, relationships, and spaces. God did not create us solely to create within the family of God, the church. What we cultivate and who we cultivate can create a storyline others want to follow. Followers of Jesus can become a redemptive alternative to the patterns of this world.

Andy Crouch pointed out, "Creativity is the only viable source of change."[13] We need apostles, prophets, evangelists, shepherds, and teachers unleashed from the church walls to cultivate the good life of the kingdom around them as they work, play, converse, eat, and create. This is an alternative our world is waiting to see.

> There are moments when all five of these responses are appropriate. There are times we must truthfully condemn, prophetically critique, wisely copy, and joyfully consume, but they must not become our posture. Our world is in need of prophetic critique, but it is best given in cultivating beautiful things: healthy families, generous companies, winsome teams and redemptive art. Cultivation gives us the platform to share about the genius behind our work. Cultivation and creation can point to our Creator. (Quoting Poets in Athens)

In Athens, the apostle Paul critiqued the surrounding culture by reframing it and creating new possibilities:

> So Paul, standing in the midst of the Areopagus, said: "Men of Athens, I perceive that in every way you are very religious. For as I passed along and observed the objects of your worship, I found also an altar with this inscription: 'To the unknown god.' What therefore you worship as unknown, this I proclaim to you. *The God who made the world and everything in it, being Lord of heaven and earth, does not live in temples made by man, nor is he served by human hands, as though he needed anything,* since he himself gives to all mankind life and breath and everything. And he made from one man every nation of mankind to live on all the face of the earth, having determined allotted periods and the boundaries of their dwelling place, *that they should seek God, and perhaps feel their way toward him and find him. Yet he is actually not far from each one of us,* for

> "'In him we live and move and have our being';[14]
> as even some of your own poets have said,
> "'For we are indeed his offspring.'"[15]
>
> (Acts 17:22–28)

Paul approaches culture uniquely in this encounter, critiquing it from the inside out. He even quotes two Greek poets as reference points to lead them toward the gospel.

Paul created an environment where culture could be the gateway and the gospel could be the spectacle. He sensed these people needed something other than a monologue that day, and he flanked them with it:

> Being then God's offspring, we ought not to think that the divine being is like gold or silver or stone, an image formed by the art and imagination of man. The times of ignorance God overlooked, but now he commands all people everywhere to repent, because he has fixed a day on which he will judge the world in righteousness by a man whom he has appointed; and of this he has given assurance to all by raising him from the dead."
>
> Now when they heard of the resurrection of the dead, *some mocked.* But others said, *"We will hear you again about this."* So Paul went out from their midst. But *some men joined him and believed.* (Acts 17:29–34)

Paul engages culture en route to creatively sharing the gospel of Jesus with them. And the people responded in three ways: some mocked, some wanted to hear more, and some believed.

You will experience these three responses most times when you proclaim truth into skepticism. We live in a skeptical world, where truth is easy to reject but relationships are hard to deny. We need to create environments, as Paul did, that can foster the following things for the sake of the gospel:

- Conversation: People want to talk through issues and bounce ideas off others. I believe the loss of table time in our homes has created a new hunger for relationship and conversation. Truth grenades aren't effective. They repel people. Instead of punching people between the eyes with truth, conversation and dialogue can remind them of the plausibility of the gospel.
- Authenticity: Our culture is hungering for things that are real. We easily sniff out inauthenticity and bad motives. We should spend some of our best energy creating space for stories, vulnerability, confession, and tragedy.
- Improvisation: People desire spaces to dream, where they don't have to be sure of results. Push against the fear of failure by creating space for it. Experiments, or pilots, create an alternative narrative to fearing failure, one that instead fears stagnancy.
- Healthy critique: People are hungry to learn and grow, but they need to be treated with dignity as they do so. People want to be part of environments and teams that hone their genius. Open up spaces in your relationships for others to critique you so you can model this. Be sure to be tactful and kind.
- Networks: People long to be meaningfully connected to others. Healthy networks bring people together to accomplish more together than they could alone. In a world where we collect large numbers of so-called friends on social media,

people are longing for a few crucial connections. Network gatherings can connect those from different tribes, spheres, or social groups to a common conversation or goal.

- Risk taking: People long for risky environments. These might involve sharing lofty dreams, asking someone to lead with vulnerability, or sharing an audacious future. I believe most Westerners today are simply bored. We need to curate contagious environments. Risks create more risks.

Churches Are Genius Labs

Churches can become genius labs. The family of God is the best space on the planet to develop leaders. We lean into risks, but our identity as children of the King is protected. Churches can be a beautiful space for development, and apprenticeship is the best tool we have. Apprenticeships are immersions into dedicated seasons of relational, experiential, and formal learning. Perhaps your church is already apprenticing leaders toward Jesus. Perhaps you have a long way to go to find an environment where apprentices can find the support and freedom to take risks. I discuss this at length in my book *Guardrails* and even finish the book with an assessment of the apprentice culture.

We must learn to celebrate growth and development, not the final product. When we are obsessed with excellence we fail to develop people. We will miss opportunities to apprentice leaders. The people around us are developing as we speak. We struggle to see our own growth. We need others to help us see it. When I was growing up, I hated family reunions. An older woman who smelled like carpet cleaner would come up and squeeze my cheeks and remind me how much I had grown since she last saw me. I was clueless who she was and would helplessly look to my parents. She hadn't seen me in years, or she was a complete stranger. I couldn't tell.

My youngest son is in kindergarten. He is a smart kid. The other day he made me a book. It made my heart swell. He is learning to read and write and comes home and makes books for me.

His latest book featured a pink man on the front: no pants, a crooked smile, terrible hair, no arms, and only one eye. I was honored to find out it was me. Inside, this future bestseller read, "MoMes R NiSe." The next page of this stirring narrative read, "DaDEs R NiSe." In a turn of events the book finished with the following: "MoMes R FUn. DaDEs R FuN." An instant classic! It stirred my heart. I absolutely loved it! Not only was I one of the only two characters in the book, but I made the front cover.

Can you imagine if I would've said to my son: "That's the worst book I've ever read. The drawing is insulting, the spelling is terrible, and the content is shallow. Writing fail!"

He's in kindergarten. He is just learning the alphabet and starting to sound out words. This is incredible development, but I'm not going to measure it next to John Grisham or J. K. Rowling.

Apprenticeships are crucial to spiritual and creative growth. If there is one area you can enhance the culture of your church in the next two years, it's apprenticeships. It's how we develop leaders from the inside and reproduce kingdom leaders. The relational, experiential, and formal learning aspects create in-time holistic learning.[16] Apprentices learn a skill through experience, among trusting relationships, while absorbing the essential knowledge on the subject.

Once I started apprenticing leaders, I never turned back. I

was hooked. It stirred the pot of meaning deep within me. It was hard and took a lot of time, but it was deeply fulfilling to teach and practice ministry alongside others.

Apprenticeships are very different from internships. Interns do menial tasks; apprentices do meaningful tasks. Interns tag along; apprentices learn a craft. Many churches have internship programs in place of hired staff. In other words, they do it for financial reasons. If you are not developing leaders to intentionally invest in them it will come up short.

Here are a few practical thoughts on apprenticeships:

- Apprentices must be given real and weighty tasks.
- Apprentices must have a safe space to fail and succeed.
- Apprentices must feel like they are part of a team.
- Apprentices must feel the freedom to fly away when the apprenticeship is over. This keeps their eyes on both the present and the future.
- Apprenticeships must be valued as growing leaders today, not "someday" leaders.
- Apprenticeships must be seen as both discipleship and leadership development.
- Apprenticeships won't bring as much value to the host as it does to the apprentice.
- Apprenticeships must be long enough to experience different seasons but short enough to bring urgency to their learning.
- Multiple apprentices can create powerful peer learning environments.
- Apprenticeships require investment, so the host must choose apprentices with care.

- Apprenticeships must be done intentionally, because apprentices will reproduce what they learned during this time.
- Look for hungry apprentices, not impressive leaders.

Practical Ideas for Fostering Genius

Create Giveaways and Grants

Each year we try to take a new risk at our annual Multiply Conference. Some work out and some don't. One of my favorite risks was called the Great Commission(al) Giveaway. The aim was to inspire creative mission–minded endeavors in local communities. We gave away three grants at the conference: $500, $1,000, and $2,000 toward innovative initiatives to serve local communities.

The creativity was amazing. A team, mostly comprised of business leaders, sifted through all the ideas, amazed at what we saw. Some were already doing great things in their communities and wanted to take it to the next level. Some simply needed the excuse of something that felt like a contest to put their idea on paper and take the risk.

The ideas ranged from specialized counseling of under-privileged families to art shows to community discussions to neighborhood dinners to business lunches. It was an excuse for people to dream, and then our team at Frontline Church Planting was allowed to validate and celebrate their ideas. One risk and a little bit of cash sparked many other creative risks. Most of those who applied, even those who did not receive any grant money, ended up carrying out their ideas and blessing their communities. I have heard of churches doing a *Shark Tank*-esque event similar to this, where small groups, ministries, and families presented *their* ideas to their church leadership and similar grants were given.

Widen the Scope of the Stories You Tell from the Stage

Expand the paradigm, share about those taking the gospel into new spheres. In his book *Unlikely*, Kevin Palau wrote, "I've found that relentlessly telling the good stories of God at work is the single best way to inspire and cast fresh vision and effort."[17] This can make its way into a show-and-tell environment, where stories become the kindling for the flames to catch.

Pastors, we need to dig around a bit to catch our people doing great stuff and share those stories. Howard Gardner echoed this when he wrote, "Leaders achieve effects primarily by telling stories and by embodying those stories in their own lives."[18] Recently a pastor at our church read a story of a woman's life transformation at a parish church. Her path to our church was through ordinary, nonpaid leaders. Everyone got to celebrate both the radical story of this woman's life change and of the couple who joined her faith journey.

Re-remind Your People of What the Church Is and Isn't

Often people are waiting for the church staff to tell them what to do. As church leaders, we need to be careful not to frame vision-casting meetings, sermon series, or church-wide initiatives as the only places where ideas are generated. Instead we need to reeducate our people to know they have unique and creative ideas. People don't need to ask permission from their church leadership to live on mission; Jesus already commissioned every believer to do that. Yep, that counts as permission.

Capture Stories on Video

Most churches accidentally go heavy on the information and light on the transformation. Our church is shifting from a focus on information about upcoming events to life transformation. It's a constant battle. Ministry leaders want their events promoted, and certainly those can be important, but a steady flow of information will slowly lull your congregation to sleep.

I discuss the tension involved in church programs in my book *Guardrails*. It takes some work, but aim to find stories of God at work and capture those stories. Videos are incredibly reproducible and can evoke the same emotion each time they are viewed.

Invite Others to Tell Their Stories on Your Site

More church websites are including stories. Often these stories are told through a blog, an interview, or a short article. These can highlight community impact, personal faith, faithful presence, neighboring, and local missions engagement.

Invite Business Leaders to Shape Environments

I like to utilize the expertise of business leaders in assessments and strategy sessions. I have found business leaders are generally comfortable talking about the potential of failure and risk. They ask great questions during church-planting assessments, and they see through different lenses than paid church leaders.

This past year I invited church planters to pitch their ideas to kingdom-minded business leaders and get feedback and criticism. I established that no partnership money was to be exchanged here, so leaders weren't competing against one another in their pitch. Everyone around the table shared for twenty minutes, and then received honest feedback for twenty minutes. They found crucial feedback before they were in a real pitch situation with a leader or committee.

Create Dream Session Environments

Make space to dream with your leadership and core teams. You will have to protect this time as you are not looking for finished products, and you won't be immediately acting on anything. One leader on our team shared how he had dreamed of his home becoming a refuge and retreat space for pastors. Other leaders shared dreams for the future of our church that they wanted to help shape. These times can be powerful!

Put People with Diverse Gifting on Your Stage

The makeup of your leadership team tells a story. If those in the seats cannot identify with anyone on the stage, they will likely shrink away from additional responsibility. It's important to put as many nonpaid church leaders on stage as you can. They might be a bit rough at first, but that's okay. The story of diverse leadership on stage is more important than excellence. Work hard to find these spaces in your services and events where new geniuses can rise to the surface. Church leaders, be ready to step out of the way to allow for team leadership. You'll be glad you did.

Reframing Hospitality

My friends Seth and Angela have had eclectic people orbiting their lives as long as I've known them. They are always bringing relationally needy folks along and adding dignity to their lives. They have met physical needs of food, clothes, and showers, but they also have sought to meet their relational needs. Angela also invites kids into discipleship opportunities providing rides to and from school. She has provided holiday meals for a home full of eclectic friends who would not normally convene. Seth and Angela take their physical neighbors as seriously as they have taken those on the fringes. They are hospitality geniuses.

We need to reframe hospitality with a greater eye for those on the fringes. Hospitality is not cooking exquisite food and vacuuming your carpet so Christians can study the Bible in your living room. This is great, but it's not the aim of biblical hospitality. If there is one genius we have misunderstood and under-understood, it's biblical hospitality. Biblical hospitality is a readiness to accept all outsiders into your life and home. The point is not to impress but to love. If hospitality is alive in our personal environment (life, home, schedule), we will eventually develop a culture of this in our collective environments (churches, businesses, teams, meetings). There are outsiders in close proximity to us all the time, we just don't see them.

Jesus was the most hospitable person who ever lived. He was always focused on outsiders and outcasts on the fringes who had no real clout or position. Parties, meals, and social spaces were bridges into personal relationship. Social outcasts entered His space just to sense His presence and power. Jesus gave them priority over the socially respected and dignified. If you find yourself completely insulated from people on the fringe, you aren't living like Jesus.

That Time God Punched Me in the Gut

I remember a moment when I realized my life had become insulated. I was reading about how to reach out to others and build bridges to the lost. I could explain a life of mission to you, I just wasn't living one. Beyond those I interacted with in my pastoral role, I had no ongoing, meaningful relationships with those who didn't know Jesus.

In a long line in a grocery store, God whispered to me, *Stop reading about it, and start doing it.* It was a gut punch I needed it. I was embarrassed. It was time to shift my priorities and the priorities of my family. During that season, I put down the book, picked up the phone, and reengaged relationships with people who didn't know Jesus.

Our family began investing differently. We rediscovered hospitality. Over time, our home shifted from a *refuge from mission* to a *hub for mission.* My greatest discovery of the last ten years of ministry has been hospitality—reclaiming the call to an open life, an open home, and an open table.

Celebrate those who understand how to include those on the fringes. Celebrate those around you who are embedded in meaningful relationships with friends and neighbors. Take every opportunity to resist the urge to solely invite Christians into your home or around your table. Follow the example of Jesus whose ministry strategy was incarnation.

DISCUSS THIS

- What practices do you have for equipping those around you for ministry?
- How has your search for excellence gotten in the way of developing others?
- Which of these words most reflects your response to culture: condemn, critique, copy, consume, or create?
- In which areas are you honing the creativity of others? Which areas can you experiment with?
- How do you celebrate those who are practicing hospitality?
- How can your ministry function more as a genius lab?

CHAPTER 8

ACCIDENTAL GENIUSES

GOD claims Earth and everything in it,
GOD claims World and all who live on it.
—Psalm 24:1 THE MESSAGE

If you are humble, nothing will touch you, neither
praise nor disgrace, because you know what you are.[1]
—Mother Teresa

What humanity needs most is for us to set creativity
free from this singular category of the extraordinary
and release it into the hands of the ordinary.[2]
—Erwin McManus

Another last-minute text from my friend. He usually only sends me these when something is really good. He's probably the most minimal texter I know. It was about life change—again. He's at the center of his community and is getting to experience God at work in the people around him.

He told me it was time to fill up the trough and baptize his friend that Sunday. We couldn't wait another week. It was a shimmering moment on Sunday morning as his friend told her story of transformation. She shared the miracles God had worked in her. We cheered a lot and cried a little. I forget what I preached about that day.

I'm a pastor, but I'm not at the center of God's vision for our faith community. God is. If I'm honest, much of my goal in moments like this is simply getting out of the way and letting others in the church family be the ministers. My friend just needed permission. He needed me to let him be who God had made him to be. Miracles unfold in our communities when we are willing to get out the way.[3]

God gives us room to cocreate with Him. He does the heavy lifting but invites us to join. Andy Crouch pointed out: "God has provided the raw material—the garden, the animals themselves and Adam's very breath. But now the Creator graciously steps back just enough to allow humankind to begin to discover what it means to be creator."[4] Think about Jesus giving the instructions of the Great Commission. He gives the *what* of ministry but lets us work out the *how*. God gives parameters, but He gives us enough freedom so every story is unique.

Every person, every team, and every church is unique. Our uniqueness involves the makeup of our leaders, gifts, heritage, experiences, traditions, values, personalities, relationships, motivations, and countless other factors.[5] We are all unique, yet we are all inherently human.

I can't wire a house. Or at least you wouldn't want me to try to wire yours. It takes an expert. But once the house is wired, plugging something in is easy. God wires the house, so to speak, and we just hook into the power source. We can do things innately only because God has wired us a certain way. Sometimes living within our genius feels as simple as plugging something in or flipping a switch. God often allows us to give off His aroma in areas in which He has deeply wired us.

Creativity in an Age of Criticism

We live in a critical world. We fear failure because we have seen others raked over the coals for it. We have seen others publicly shamed when a risk didn't turn out. Our culture is more critical than it is creative. Michelangelo's modus operandi—"Criticize by creating"—would serve us well today. We need more creating and less criticizing. There are careers in filmmaking and directing, but there are also careers as a film critic. As Christian leaders, we must lean more toward creation than critique. God Himself is our example of creation. The Creation narrative ended with "It was good," not "It used to be bad."

Plenty of creatives are dreamers. This can be good or bad. A dream can develop into something more when we realize it is a God-given calling. Creatives and dreamers can take great faith risks by looking beyond the *what* to remember *why* they do what they do and *who* they do it for.[6] Faith isn't about crafting a strategic ten-step plan; it's about taking the next right step. People labeled as creatives tend to inspire us. Many of them have taken risks we wish we had the faith to take ourselves. Good creativity should be rooted in good theology.

Servants Who Sometimes Lead

The late Henri Nouwen had much to say about leadership in our confusing world. He described it as a descent into servanthood, not an ascent into power.[7] Nouwen practiced what he preached by leaving the respect he had garnered as an Ivy League professor to work with those who had intellectual disabilities. The genius that had been recognized and affirmed in one area of society was worthless in another. His life was a lesson in downward mobility to the cross.

Leadership is one of the tensions we must live in. We are servants of the living God, but we all possess genius that is valuable in this world. First, we must be servants, and second, we must be leaders. If leadership is influence, as John Maxwell has famously defined it, then it's truly about bringing others on mission with us. Christian leaders are, first, followers of Jesus and, second, leaders of others. We need to affirm others for the unique genius they possess while reminding those we lead how to embody humility.

Play—Passion—Purpose

Chuck is a solid guy in our church. He is a supportive husband and a loving father. He works in the defense industry, makes business attire look good, and he's good with numbers. I've been watching God grow Chuck, and I sensed it was time to get together and lean in. Over coffee, I shared what I saw in him—the man, father, and husband he was. I let him know I believed in him and saw great potential in him.

After a few busy weeks at work, he walked up to me in the hall after a Sunday service. He wanted to talk. This can mean any number of things to a pastor, so I usually get a lump in my throat when I hear this. Chuck cut to the chase. He wanted to talk about how he could find his sweet spot in leadership and ministry. He was hungry and ready, but he wanted some guidance.

I am excited to play the role of coach and cheerleader (minus the pom-poms) in Chuck's life. Chuck would be faithful to fill any role we have for him, but I want to help guide him into areas he connects with. I want to help Chuck find an area of passion and purpose he can invest in.

Tony Wagner believes there are three interrelated elements that drive every person: play, passion, and purpose.[8] These three areas spring straight from the heart of God. Play expresses joy: the joy of creation and the joy we are meant to experience in rest and re-creation. Play has a very high value in Colorado. We take our play seriously, and we work hard to get it.

My friend Joe started roasting coffee because he loves it. He cleared out a shed and started to experiment. Quickly, something he did for fun turned into a recognized commodity in our town. What started as play for Joe is clearly a passion, and he is starting to wonder how it can impact greater purposes in our city and beyond. Now I get to sit at a local shop and enjoy a fine Ethiopian pourover straight from the heart of Joe.

If people can find joy in doing something (play), they can find the desire to keep doing it (passion). When someone is passionate about something, we should engage them with questions.

- Why are you so passionate about this?
- What is it about this activity that connects so deeply with you?
- What possibilities can you explore to empower others through this?

People find the time and money to invest in their passions, and they like to talk about them. We can help to validate others' creativity by helping them find purpose in it. Many people are one simple step away from applying themselves to a particular area and excelling in it. How can you help others find a divine purpose in what they're already doing?

Seth Godin noted, "When you talk to people who are committed to their art, what you'll discover is this; they never stop giving."[9] It's innate. Passion comes from God. We can't cook up a batch of passion. There's no recipe for it. Passion of any flavor requires discernment. The challenge is not to become more passionate but to become more purposeful with the passion we've been given. Passion must always be channeled.

There is always passion behind purpose, a way to use the things we love for the sake of the world. God designed us to be givers not takers, investors not consumers. As we often refer to Jesus's journey to the cross as the Passion, He was actually living out His purpose to lay His life down for all humanity. Throughout the Gospels, Jesus is a model for purpose. Jesus was constantly extending compassion in His encounters and asking the disciples to do the same.

In Genesis, God asked Abraham to give up his earthly rights in order to be a blessing to the world. We don't exist to be a genius; we exist to be generous. Followers of Jesus should be the most giving people on the planet: giving away freely and blessing the socks off those around us. Any genius we have isn't to make *us* famous but to make *Him* famous.

Passion is what makes people stay up late, hop out of bed early, or invest their spare time and money. In his book *Outliers*, Malcolm Gladwell tells the story of Bill Gates and Paul Allen sneaking out and writing computer code that led to both the founding of Microsoft and the digital revolution. Passion is what keeps musicians playing in a garage band, learners taking courses for fun in their spare time, and people investing inordinate amounts of time to serve others. Passion can always be redirected, honed, and disciplined, but it cannot be created. It is given by God alone. Play *plus* passion *plus* purpose *equals* a recipe to unleash God's people into greater impact.

Money's Always Getting in the Way

"How do I make a living doing this?" Most of us have to ask this question about our passions or dreams at some point. Sometimes making a living can be a real pain. Some have followed this question down the rabbit hole, concluding they couldn't make a living with their craft and they would have to support their habit on the side. Some have struck gold and felt they were paid for what they would do for free.

Whatever camp you find yourself in, camp well.
Live intentionally.
Keep creating and risking.

My friend Jon seems he is in a paid ministry position. He's not. He brokers mortgages for a living, but he has learned to free his time for ministry pursuits. Jon serves God all week, sometimes through leading ministries and sometimes as a ministering lender.

A friend sat in one of his favorite cafés in San Francisco. He loved looking at a mural on the wall at the shop as he sipped a latte. One day he learned the artist who painted it was in the shop.

"What do you do," he asked.

She said, "I'm an artist."

He began to ask her about the inspiration for her work and how she makes a living as an artist.

"Oh no, it's not my job," she clarified. *Artist* is a deep part of her identity, but she never needed to make a dollar doing it in order to validate that.

Our deepest creativity does not have to make its way into a career or even a side job. I called a retired physicist to see if his jazz-and-funk band would be available for an event.

He said, "We don't charge. We don't need to do that."

There is something about creativity that keeps us coming back if we never get paid a dollar for doing it. It is not more or less pure to charge for our creativity. The pull of serving God with our whole hearts is greater than the pull of bringing in a paycheck. What you are willing to do for free says a lot about your passion.

Do I Have What It Takes?

My friend Mike was making a good living but found himself longing to take the leap to start a business helping other businesses to succeed. He found himself putting in his notice at his steady job (with a baby on the way) because he absolutely knew it was time to focus on his passion with a majority of his energy.

He said: "I needed to do this because it was how I could be *fully* alive, fully alive as a whole person professionally, spiritually, personally. I knew that if I didn't do it I would have huge regrets and what-ifs. I knew that God was calling me to take a risk that I knew would fail without divine intervention."

Leaning into creativity can be terrifying. Erwin McManus

highlighted the inherent risk of the creative process: "There is an order to the creative process: we dream, we risk, we create."[10]

Mike's story reminds us of the risk of creativity.

He was terrified as he took this risk but excited about the possibilities. He asked himself, "Do I really have what it takes to do this?" We are all asking this question.

Mike said: "Nothing caused me more to get on my knees and become fully dependent upon the Father as taking this risk did. I can truly say that this risk has caused more growth in my life spiritually with Jesus, intimacy with my wife, and seeing firsthand I truly trust the Father as my provider. There has been monumental growth for me the past three years."

There is no template. Every story is unique, but we are all considering our next risk. Mike's challenge to others who are thinking about taking a major risk is this: "When we fail to take action, we forfeit the future. Just as inaction is an action, indecision is a decision. You must be released from and called out before you can make that leap. You can't just pray as if it depends solely on God; you also have to work as if it depends on you."

Conversations with leaders like Mike make me feel fully alive. In fact, these conversations with leaders on the edge of risk led me to begin life coaching. They remind me of the moments I stood at the edge of a massive risk, saying, "God, I hope You've got this!" I love to sit with leaders weighing options and testing the depth of the water below the cliff they are peeking over.

In the course of a month I talk with many leaders about their next season or next risk. God's people should be courageous but also discerning. We can't do this alone. If you're at the edge of a cliff, bring your idea to others. Church leaders, when someone comes to you with a faith risk, they need your advice, but they need your affirmation even more. They need you to remind them of a creative and loving Father who created them in His image. Remind them they are not defined by what they do or don't do but instead by the love of the Father.

Sprouting Creativity

I attended a Southern prep school. The culture was *driven*. I was a jock. Sports was what I did, but it was also who I was. I thought artists were weird. They were doodling on the margins of the page. I didn't understand them, but they seemed to be really into it. They were tucked away in the art room while everyone else was having fun. I only visited there occasionally to get a hug from Lisa, a cute girl who seemed to have an apartment there. At the age of sixteen, I concluded: *I am not an artist, and I don't I want to be.*

On a whim one evening ten years later, I decided to drive to an art supply store, pick up some canvases, and paint. I know. It was a wild Friday-night plan. I woke up from a painting trance at about 3 a.m. I was hooked. I loved it! As I look back at that moment, it didn't produce a new flavor of creativity in me, but it allowed me to peer at life through acrylic paint on a canvas. At the time, I was finally growing into my love of reading, but I still hated to write. I still resisted the word *artist*, but I have always been creative. Most people would not call themselves artists, but everyone has creativity ready to be released. It only needs to be validated, encouraged, and given a chance to blossom.

There are jobs and roles that seem to become popular overnight. Life coaches, coffee educators, nutrition consultants, spiritual directors, curators, and cultural directors are examples of new fields that have quickly arisen over the last few years. There are scores of new opportunities to impact others and build relationships.

Taste and See (and Smell) That God Is Good

A young believer I met in Turkey shared his conversion story with me. He grew up as a secular Muslim. He walked the same busy street each day on his way to work. Each day when he passed a certain storefront, he smelled flowers, but there was no flower shop in sight. One day he simply had to figure out where this smell was coming from. He entered the store front to find out it was an undercover church building, where followers of Jesus regularly gathered for prayer. He saw no flowers, and no one was wearing perfume. He learned about Jesus through those believers for the next several days. One evening, in a dream, he saw Jesus calling from the cross for him to come.

God is at work in our world, spreading His aroma through His people.

Paul's second letter to the church in Corinth says: "Thanks be to God, who in Christ always leads us in triumphal procession, and through us spreads the fragrance of the knowledge of him everywhere. For we are the aroma of Christ to God among those who are being saved and among those who are perishing, to one a fragrance from death to death, to the other a fragrance from life to life" (2 Cor. 2:14–16).

Followers of Jesus are to be a sweet aroma to the world, spreading the fame of Jesus. We should smell like a campfire to an outdoorsman, barbecue to a meat lover, flowers to a gardener, fresh bread to a hungry traveler, and cotton candy to a child. God releases His people to be His sweet aroma of freedom to a world living in the stench of slavery. Empower others to live for Jesus as they are wired and gifted. Open the doors of the church building to watch an empowered people reach others in unique ways. Smell how the spirit of the living God is at work in the community around you.

Three Things People Are Seeking

I have observed three prevailing desires people are seeking in the local church today. I don't usually see this right away, but after a while it usually emerges.

Convenience

Many people are looking for the fastest, easiest way to get in and get out of church gatherings. They are looking for minimal work and time, but they want a feel-good factor. Convenience of drive time, shortness of the service, and ideal gathering time must be achieved to keep these folks on board. They are looking for the most succinct packaging available. When you are in the middle of a busy day and need to put food in your belly, you look for the fastest food option you can find. But convenience doesn't lead to spiritual nourishment.

Consumption

Others are looking to drink deep of the church experience. This will likely drive them to look for the best possible programs for them and their families. The desires differ from person to person, but they view the church as a dispenser of religious goods, and they are looking for the finest goods around. This can look much deeper on the surface as they readily take notes during sermons and compliment church leadership on a recent event or sermon series.

I hear stories of families who attended churches for years and suddenly stop attending. It's as if they suddenly fell out of love with the style and programs of the church. The adage "whatever you win them with, you will have to keep them with" should be a warning to us for those simply looking to consume what a church has to offer. At some level the desire to consume a church and its offerings is misunderstood ecclesiology, a confusion of what Jesus' church is.

Investment

There is a group of people in every church who gets it. Some have labeled this the 20 percent that does 80 percent of the work, but I call them the investors. While I have heard countless church leaders get angry at the 20/80 rule, I think this is going to be a reality in most places. Not everyone is hungry. Not everyone is ready to invest.

This isn't just in North America, but this is true in many discipling relationships across the globe.[11] This was true with Jesus's focus on pulling Peter, James, and John closer than the other disciples before the church was launched. They were the deepest investors among the disciples. Look for the hungry. Look for those who stay after events and clean up. Look for those who are doing things when they aren't told to do them. Look for those who are applying God's words to their lives. Look for those serving in the children's ministry without being shamed into it. Look for those taking risks outside the walls of the church.

When you spy investors in your church, you need to *invest* in them! We need to spend some of our best time equipping these leaders. I'm not saying that others are unspiritual or not worthy of our time, but I am saying we often have our eyes on the masses instead of on the few. Perhaps one in every five people in your congregation is hungry and ready to be equipped and coached into living out their genius. Work to create a funnel system for effectively using your time and focusing on the call to "equip the saints for the work of ministry" (Eph. 4:12).

Choose Life So Your Gifts Bless

Too often we use our gifts as weapons. It grieves me to watch Christians holding their gifts in front of others in a showy way (even if it's disguised as a humble brag) or seeking public validation. I often watch Christ followers use their intelligence to slam others in theological arguments. Sometimes I catch myself name-dropping or needlessly sharing accomplishments and needing a gut check from God. The Lord speaks to this:

> I call heaven and earth to witness against you today, that I have set before you life and death, blessing and curse. Therefore *choose life*, that you and your offspring may live, loving the LORD your God, obeying his voice and holding fast to him, for *he is your life and length of days*, that you may dwell in the land that the LORD swore to your fathers, to Abraham, to Isaac, and to Jacob, to give them. (Deut. 30:19–20)

Choose life with your gifts and talents. Throwing your gifts in the face of others tears us apart instead of binding the body together.

The temptations are great. Humility is the narrow road in a culture bent on building ourselves up so I can look down on others.

Don't Be a Hoarder

If you've ever watched a special on hoarders it's hard to imagine why anyone would have the desire to hang onto so much stuff. As church leaders we have some hoarding issues too. We don't own those in our churches, but sometimes we act like we do. We need to release people to live out their gifting, not hoard them and their gifts. The gifts, personality, and wiring of each person was given by God for the sake of the world.

Kevin Palau issued a warning here: "If we're not careful, we can end up hoarding disciples, challenging them to primarily apply their gifts within the confines of the church body instead of encouraging them and equipping them to be the best bankers they can be for the community. Of course we need to keep our local churches functioning, but maintaining our church programs is not the primary way the kingdom gets built! Unleashing the creativity and expertise of every disciple, empowering them to engage in the community makes all the difference."[12]

In order to feed movement outward into our needy communities (yes, every community is needy), church leaders must view the gifts our people possess as assets God wants to bless our communities with. These people can be gifts to our community. God has bottled gifts inside of each of them, waiting to be cracked open. If our vantage doesn't exceed the size of our church, then our impact will never exceed the size of our church either.

A church in the Northwest has an artist collective that

meets monthly to challenge one another to continue to create beautiful art that impacts their city. Artists need encouragement. They live on the fringes and take many risks on a daily basis. They've created an affirming and encouraging space. This doesn't mean they are looking for art to beef up their lobby walls or fill their services. It means they are affirming what people are already doing in the community. How can your church inspire each person to repurpose their gifts for the sake of your community?

God Doesn't Work Accidentally

Just the other day a friend told me an amazing story of God at work. She had been carefully and intentionally walking closely with a friend for a few years. She asked us to pray for her friend often. Her friend was resistant to the gospel and to the church but very open to relationships.

One day her friend experienced so much pain in her life that she broke. She drove to my friend's house in crisis mode. Over the next few hours God surrounded her with His love through a house full of friends. She stepped over the line of faith toward Jesus that night at the kitchen table.

They all realized what was unfolding. The smell of fresh bread wafted from the oven. The girls had been sitting around the table sipping wine. This woman's first act of obedience was to experience communion around a dinner table. Taste and see that the Lord is good! God is not working through accidents. He orders our lives and our impact. This story has been unfolding for a long time, but we get invited in later in the story.

Pillars of Jesus in a Community

My mechanic is also my friend. Because we drive older cars, I see him at the garage more than I would like. I should probably start sending them Christmas cards. He is a good mechanic, but he's an even better caretaker. When you walk in with a car issue, you find yourself vulnerable, frustrated, and tight on cash. I know as little about cars as I do about physics. He has diagnosed issues and fixed our cars many times. He has empathy. He knows what it's like to have your back against the wall.

One day when I was waiting for my car to be fixed, I noticed a comment board. There were thank-you notes, many of them directed to "G." One lady even referred to him as "her angel." I asked G what this was all about. He told me about a woman with very little money coming in with bald tires. He found some used tires that would do the trick and didn't charge her. He saved the day for her.

G is right where he needs to be: serving people. He is the same guy at church gatherings where he finds others are struggling. He's a caretaker who happens to be a mechanic. G might find himself serving in a caretaking capacity someday within the walls of our church, but he is a caretaker in our community right now. He has served numbers of my friends in vulnerable and frustrated moments. He is shining the light of Jesus in an area we would rarely call ministry. There are geniuses like G already living out their call for Jesus at this very moment.

When pastors bless and affirm the work of a congregation outside of the walls and programs of a church, they are often greeted with surprise. Many pastors fear releasing people into opportunities outside of church programs. We fear that putting an emphasis somewhere other than the church might be bad for church business. Congregations might even be surprised when their pastor releases them to passionately do something *out there*. That could crack open the window of possibility. It could release them to their God-given genius.

Surprise your people. Release them to the work that is waiting for them in the community or affirm what they are already doing.

Andrew and Hannah are incredibly talented: drama, script-writing, choreography, you name it. Two right brains married each other. They are a creative power couple. They regularly produce and hone things that simply make the rest of us feel downright boring. They are artists to the core. Their gifts have been utilized at times inside our church programs, but they will rarely fit there. Their stages are shaped differently, and their gifts shine more clearly outside the walls.

They have never come to me for new creative ideas in their career. But they need other things: life advice, encouragement to keep going, and affirmation that they are built for what they are doing. Some of the most creative folks have slipped through our fingers in the church or at least gone under our radar. They can get into unique niches that no one else around them can.

Who are the pillars of Jesus in your community? Some of those around you are already living for the sake of the world. Others are ready to start. Find them. Affirm them. Unleash them.

DISCUSS THIS

- Who are a few pillars of Jesus in your community you can affirm?

- In which ways can you use your genius to be generous?
- What does your view of creativity say about your theology?
- How can you encourage others to use their genius to be generous?
- In which areas are you most tempted to use your gifts as weapons instead of blessings?
- Where do play, passion, and purpose align in your life and ministry?

CHAPTER 9

UNLEASHING GENIUSES

Originality is fragile.[1]

—Ed Catmull

If the church exists for the world, then the people in our churches exist for the world. We don't own them. They belong to Jesus. The job of those who may pastor or lead is to release them to the world.[2]

—Kevin Palau

It's hard to copy something you can't see.[3]

—Jonah Berger

By the time he was twenty-six, David had a net worth of four million dollars. He was making a quarter of a million dollars a year. (That's more than twenty thousand dollars a month.) Life looked pretty good at that point, but over the next few years Dave lost it all. He had been silently fighting debt, and no one around him had any idea.

He went back to the drawing board, learning how to acquire money through real estate and take control of his life. He spent time learning from rich people who knew how to hold on to their money. His search made him reexamine himself and his habits. He wanted to do more than make money; he wanted to help others walk the same path he had walked from the chasm of debt.

His name is Dave Ramsey. Ever heard of him? He began selling copies of his book, *Financial Peace,* out of his car. Today, he has had six *New York Times* bestsellers to his credit, he hosts the hit radio program *The Dave Ramsey Show,* and he regularly fills stadiums with anxious listeners. All of this is en route to helping others get their finances healthy. He measures success in terms of transformation.[4] Dave loves Jesus, and he has been given a massive platform to teach biblical principles and share his faith. God has used him to transform millions of people and free them from financial slavery.

Most opportunities don't look golden at first. God often chooses to birth beauty out of struggle. Many stories only make sense when you read them backward. For a season our family was struggling financially, and it forced me to get a side job. It felt like failure to have to work two jobs to provide for my family. In that time I was able to have conversations with hundreds of high schoolers inside public school classrooms about making healthy choices as I sprinkled the gospel into my teaching.

A friend of mine hit rock bottom financially. Out of desperation he took a job that felt menial and barely paid his bills. But through this monotonous job, he came up with an idea to launch a business that could support his family and pay his mortgage. His business took off. Every week he interacts with hundreds of leaders, local universities, and businesses all over the city as he continues to minister through a local church.

A friend spent time in prison before coming to know Jesus. He is now a pastor, husband, and father. After moving to my city to plant a church, he realized he needed to generate more income. Starting a church in the underserved south side isn't exactly a great career move, but it's what God told him to do. Through his firsthand understanding of what disadvantages people experience after being released from prison, my friend began to hire felons who were struggling to find work. Plan B turned into an opportunity. As the adage goes, scarcity brings clarity.

God has many paths to unleash geniuses. Many of them don't make sense. We need to keep our eyes open to recognize when God is doing something unique in our lives and through the lives of those around us. God has a way of creatively shaping our stories to bring Him glory.

It's Still About Discipleship

"I just want to talk to a human!" I yelled at the electronic voice prompting through a phone call. I had turned a forty-five-second question into a forty-five-minute temper tantrum. I was tired of choosing which of the seven options was best for me. I was in phone purgatory, on hold with a company that apparently hires only robots.

Our world has mechanized nearly everything in the name of efficiency. We spend much less time talking on our phones and much more time typing on our phones, mesmerized by its magical blue glow.

I have come to appreciate human interaction more than ever. A slow cup of coffee with a friend is a gift. A slow meal with my family keeps us connected through the chaos of six humans fighting to get their way. A slow stroll with my wife pulls thoughts out of us we didn't even know we were thinking. God had our humanity in mind when He made us and when He created work for us.

Jesus commissioned frail humans. He invited all of humanity who calls Him Lord through the Great Commission. This call to recognize genius is not a move away from discipleship but a call to creatively reengage discipleship. We are not inventing something new; we are seeking to recover the ways of being disciples that we have forgotten over time and translate them to a rapidly changing age.[5] Discipleship will never go out of style, and perhaps passionate disciples are needed more today than ever before.

Every follower of Jesus is in the people business. Ed Catmull of Pixar Animation attributes much of the company's massive success to its focus on their people over their product. He said, "It is the focus on people—their work habits, their talents, their values—that is absolutely central to any creative venture."[6]

Churches are in the people business. We must remind our people God loves them, He created them in His image, we love them, and they have great value. If we don't do this, we will fail to impact communities. No one wants to be used, but everyone longs to be utilized.

Many church leaders forget to affirm others, because they struggle to believe their own value. Henri Nouwen said: "One of the main sufferings experienced in the ministry is that of low self-esteem. Many priests and ministers today increasingly perceive themselves as having very little impact. They are very busy, but they do not see much change. It seems that their efforts are fruitless."[7]

God often reminds me that my impact is, indeed, limited. If I focus on myself and use faulty phrases like "my ministry," I forget what God can unleash through others. There are others around us whom God wants to utilize in His kingdom work. Many people who don't fit within the traditional paradigms of the church are highly creative and highly influential. These creatives and entertainers who make art, music, and film often "feel their calling is out of tune with their Christian upbringing. They think the church doesn't know what to do with them."[8] We need to remind them that they are gifted missionaries touched and sent by the living God.

James K. A. Smith said, "This church's mission is to send out innovators and designers whose actions aim at changing existing situations into preferred ones."[9] In short, the people of Jesus need to create an alternative picture that looks more like the hope of God's sprouting kingdom than the weary kingdom of this world.

One of the best ways church leaders can guide artists is to connect them. The life of a creative can be lonely. It can be hard to see things no one else sees. Over the ages guilds have formed powerful relational and economic bonds for artists to practice their craft. Today, artist collectives, formal and informal, exist in our cities, connecting artists to meaning and to groups of people who understand them and their work. Artists need to find other artists. As church leaders, we can link artists, especially artists of faith, who are driven by the *imago dei* as they create and recreate beauty.[10]

My friend is a connector of artists and musicians in his underrated city. He said this:

> Many disciples in a city desire a great apostolic movement, but the artists lack the unity in telling a unified kingdom story that could define their work. In John 17, Jesus prayed that His disciples would be one as He and the Father were one. As an artist, promoting community among other artists

is a beautiful and tangible way of inviting the kingdom into my work and my life. Even if I'm not collaborating with other believers, there's something about that kind of togetherness in which we see the heart of Jesus.

One of the greatest needs of this hour in the church is collaboration. Leaders need to meaningfully and humbly work together. Churches need to work together with other churches to fly the kingdom banner as *one* church in a city. Churches need to partner with organizations already doing great work in their community instead of trying to reinvent programs and processes that are already working. Collaboration can be hard. It takes significant doses of humility to realize we can accomplish more with others than we can accomplish on our own. Collaboration is also really good. It can multiply impact, increase our humility, and bring back joy where we once experienced stress. Leading alone has limits; we can only go so far and for so long. Each year that passes I realize more of my limitations, and I get a little more obsessed with the power of team.

Collaboration can unleash the full potential in leaders, churches, and organizations. This won't happen by accident. It happens through careful cultivation. Here is the progression from friendship to collaboration:

Friendship >> Partnership >> Collaboration

Friendship Yields Trust

Friendships are hugely important for any kingdom leader. We need others who can identify with us. Friendships run on the currency of trust. Trust is built through relationships where accidental competitors become friends. One pastor wasn't excited about a new church planter because folks were migrating from his established church toward the new church plant. The pastor reached out to the planter: "We need to get together so I can stop hating you." Now, many years later, they are great friends.

Magic Johnson and Larry Bird were fierce rivals during their NBA careers, but they became friends over the dinner table in Bird's rural Indiana home. Competition drives us to think the worst about someone. As we connect and interact with others, barriers come down and friendships emerge. Isolated leaders become jealous leaders. Ministry is hard. Don't do it alone.

Partnership Yields Shared Ownership

The trust forged in friendship often leads to a desire for something deeper. Leaders become motivated to work together with other leaders, churches, and organizations. They identify cracks of brokenness in their place and pray, dream, and scheme how gospel work can become the mortar that fills those cracks. Leaders might find themselves partnering on an initiative when they gather several churches to work toward a common goal. One leader usually functions as the gatekeeper leading the charge, and others join in. The currency of partnership is shared ownership. Those involved need to have some skin in the game. These partnering leaders begin to experience a deeper collective impact than they could have experienced alone.

Collaboration Yields Cocreation

The search for something deeper leads to collaboration. This moves beyond shared action to co-creation. This is where it really gets fun. In my experience, this stage is rare. When leaders and organizations collaborate, they get to co-create. It takes a long time and wise planning to get here. Motives and mission have to be checked. You can't skip friendship and partnership to get to collaboration without it getting weird. There is shared ownership in the whole process.

We need a few shots of humility if we are going to share influence, stages, processes, and resources. Pride kills collaboration. If you think you can do this better on your own or you have to control a process, you won't collaborate. Collaboration is humility in action that results in impact. When collaboration is done well, the genius of each party is realized. Collaborators don't become twice as effective; they become one hundred times more effective. It's a lot like a healthy marriage. My wife has strengths where I have weaknesses and vice versa. Together we can accomplish things we never would have attempted alone.

Forge friendship, develop partnerships, lean into collaboration, and watch kingdom impact grow. God moves through teams, and He will show Himself more effectively and creatively when leaders work together.

Collaboration in the name of the gospel tells the story of one kingdom and one church. The more kingdom collaboration that develops in our cities, the more geniuses we can get into the game. We can deploy more people faithfully into our communities.

John 17:20–23 is a cry for unity in the church:

> I'm praying not only for them
> But also for those who will believe in me
> Because of them and their witness about me.
> The goal is for all of them to become one heart and mind—

Just as you, Father, are in me and I in you,

So they might be one heart and mind with us.

Then the world might believe that you, in fact, sent me.

The same glory you gave me, I gave them,

So they'll be as unified and together as we are—

I in them and you in me.

Then they'll be mature in this oneness,

And *give the godless world evidence*

That you've sent me and loved them

In the same way you've loved me. (THE MESSAGE)

This unity also serves as a powerful apologetic: that it might "give the godless world evidence that you've sent me and loved them." In today's world, collaboration is a given. The church is positioned to lead the way in this. When we work together, we point to a God who sent us and a God who loves the world.

Healthy Teams Multiply Genius

Collaboration is steadily happening through teams. In fact, we are witnessing the rebirth of teams. The word *team* has officially left the sports arena and entered businesses, nonprofits, and churches. Teams are forming in exciting ways. Teaching teams are multiplying the preaching impact in churches. Ministry teams share the load of planning and execution. Care teams inhabit multihousing communities, showing the tangible love of Jesus. Leadership, pastoral, and executive teams discern together the work of the Spirt and the needs of a church. Creative teams design the inception of a biblical concept or sermon series into the hearts of a congregation. Executive teams guide organizations from the trenches.

Here is a simple equation I use for effective teams.

Trust + Shared Ownership + Cocreation = Effective Team

Healthy teams can multiply genius, but unhealthy teams can diminish genius. An unhealthy team can squelch the most creative ideas. At times we have an obsession with creating teams, boards, and committees simply because it feels right to do so. But we shouldn't form teams for the sake of having teams; we should form teams so we can be more effective together. Effective teams overcome our weaknesses and release our strengths into the journey of friendship, partnership, and collaboration. Teams allow us to live as a greater whole while taking our work to the next level. We need healthy, kingdom-focused teams today more than ever.

Six Marks of Healthy Teams

Healthy Teams Partner with Each Member

Those on a healthy team know people have their back and their front. Healthy teams take the time to discern the best person to lead a task or a project. Healthy teams hear leaders out when they believe they are in the wrong seat on the bus or leading in too many areas. I have gone to my team feeling overwhelmed, and they have taken things off my plate. I have moved out of the driver's seat in some areas and into the driver's seat in others.

Healthy Teams Keep Learning

Growing healthy as a team isn't a destination; it's an ever-changing journey. Healthy teams are always learning and growing individually and collectively. They are always seeking to understand one another deeper, learning more about their craft, reading on related topics, and applying new ideas for the next time. This might seem exhausting, and sometimes it is. But it has the potential to take the organization and each person to the next level.

Healthy Teams Tell the Truth

Others see the good and bad in us that we don't see in ourselves. Healthy teammates affirm what other team members do well. They also must tell what dysfunction or issues we have. In their book *Thanks for the Feedback*, Douglas Stone and Sheila Heen wrote: "Of course, YOU don't have blind spots, but you know that your colleagues, family and friends certainly do. That's the nature of blind spots. We're only blind to certain things about ourselves; we're also blind to the fact that we're blind."[11]

We tell the truth not to wound others or to feel superior but to give a better picture of reality that can lead to a preferred future. Recently a teammate shared how I had accidentally hurt him. It was painful to hear, but once he explained it to me, I understood why this was hurtful. This conversation changed me. It gave me a mirror to see myself from a different angle.

Healthy Teams Celebrate Progress

Healthy teams are always up against an obstacle, even if the obstacle is the status quo. This uphill battle of leadership grinds leaders down. Celebrating progress is a calming balm on the aches and pains of a team. These are the moments that remind us that what we're doing is worth it. Ann McGee Cooper observed: "Celebrate any progress. Don't wait to get perfect."[12] Make it a practice to celebrate the little gains and watch team morale rise.

Healthy Teams Listen

Listening is a massive part of being on a team. We must listen to God and one another. Often you have to listen through the noise or the agenda to catch glimpses of what's going on below the surface. There are whispers of passion and pain below our voices and our agendas. Parker Palmer pointed out the importance of listening: "Vocation does not come from willfulness. It comes from listening."[13] Many times we are trying to find ourselves by willing our way into the story when really we would do better to listen our way into the story.

Healthy Teams Tell Stories

Stories can affirm the members of a team. Tell on people who are doing good things! Stories have power, serious power. They are probably our greatest tool to affirm those around us and set a standard. Stories hold a social currency and release inspiration. Jonah Berger noted: "Today there are thousands of entertainment options, but our tendency to tell stories remains. We get together around our proverbial campfires—now water coolers or girls' or guys' night out—and tell stories."[14]

We must learn to mine for stories, digging below the surface of the lives and conversations of those around us. We must learn to tell and retell stories of God's people being released into the world. A sending God releases obedient people to experience transformation.

Remember, healthy teams multiply genius, and the six marks

of a healthy team are partnership, learning, truth, celebration, listening, and storytelling.

Which of these elements are present on your team?

Which of these is missing from your team?

How can you make these regular practices on your team?

The Power of Collaboration

I love visiting churches. There's a quirky diversity I like to spy for in each church. When I visit churches, I find all kinds of different marks: international impact, hospitality, neighboring, church planting, discipleship, prayer, innovation, liturgy, and care for the poor. Just like every person is a genius, every church is a genius.

When churches enter into relationship with one another and collaborate in ministry, the world will notice. The aim of mission-hearted unity in John 17 reminds us that others around us will tangibly experience the love of the Father and truly believe they are loved. When people become effective teams of missionaries, shepherds, and loving neighbors, cities notice. Schools will notice. Police departments will notice. Neighbors will notice. Other churches will notice and want to join in the fun too.

I love hearing about what some friends experienced in Denver. Many churches collaborated to cannonball into neighboring and serving their city. Dave Runyon and Jay Pathak tell the story in *The Art of Neighboring.* I am watching something similar unfold in our city through a faceless movement called #COSILoveYou. Similar movements are going on in cities across the country and world.

I got to sit down with Kevin Palau and other Portland leaders to hear how longevity and faithful presence are slowly changing

Portland. You can read about this in the book *Unlikely*. Trinity Grace Church functions like a network bringing life and flavor to New York City. Jon Tyson calls the church to embrace both faithful presence and fruitful presence in his compelling book *A Creative Minority*. When we collaborate and no one gets the credit, people will see our God. Often we collaborate, but we try to take credit. A friend calls this "spiritual photobombing."

God is the hero of the story, not us. We aren't even ghost writers. We are auxiliary characters inserted by God into the story.[15] We can't give God the glory and function as the hero of the story; we need to choose.

Equipping Leaders with Survival Skills

Tony Wagner has compiled seven survival skills he believes are necessary in today's increasingly flat world.[16] These can be incredibly helpful as we prepare kingdom leaders for influence in an ever-changing culture.

Critical Thinking and Problem Solving

We can help others develop cultural discernment and practical wisdom in everyday life. This can help people navigate the choppy waters of our culture en route to shaping their vocation and Christian witness. The pages of Proverbs are full of lessons in discernment.

Collaboration Across Networks and Leading by Influence

This is crucial for building networks with other Christ followers of different faith tribes. We need leaders who can catalyze relationships into collaboration. We can help serve our cities and ensure the local church is creating value and filling needs. Leading by influence will never go out of style. As we model our lives after *the* great servant, Jesus Himself, we have a great opportunity to show hope to our world through a leadership style that gently influences people toward hope, not hammering a top-down corporate influence that our world has put so much stock in.

Agility and Adaptability

Christians should learn to exercise the muscles of adaptation. The Holy Spirit often prompts us to change the way we live and lead. As missionaries in a post-Christian culture, we should be ready to go outside the proverbial box, busting our comfort bubble and attempting new things.

Initiative and Entrepreneurship

Often entrepreneurial wiring indicates a more apostolic gifting from God. Using the word *apostolic* might sound strange at first, but it indicates a spiritual entrepreneur.[17] In my role of directing a church planting network, I get to work with people who are innovating in the name of Jesus. Instead of asking why, they ask why not.

Entrepreneurs are serial starters; they always have the next idea in their back pocket and somehow learn how to make it come to life. We need to validate spiritual entrepreneurs. Entrepreneurship is highly valued in our world today, but we often struggle to know how to best support these folks. We will need to let them lead in a new way and validate them for coloring outside the lines. These folks can help the church make a scene for Jesus in our communities.

Accessing and Analyzing Information

We are experiencing information overload. The problem is not in finding enough information but in finding the right information. Between countless translations of Scripture and endless stacks of books, we need others to help us access and translate the information that can help us to more effectively live a Christian witness. Sorting through information to find the gems of transformation is a skill we simply must learn or we will find ourselves feeling overwhelmed and underprepared.

Effective Oral and Written Communication

We have never had more avenues for influencing others through the spoken and written word. While most people will never become professors or authors, the written and spoken word will always be powerful. From art presentations to company meetings to blogging to e-mail newsletters, clear communication is crucial. Everyone has a voice, but we all must learn to express it differently. Whether written or oral, whether leading Bible studies or meetings, these are crucial skills to cultivate.

Curiosity and Imagination

Hope forms the foundation for curiosity and imagination. Our firm foundation in the hope of Jesus should lead us to a robust imagination. This hope should have us asking, *"What if?" What if we served our community in this way? What if we tried this idea? What if we could meet this crucial need? What if we could create culture in this sphere?*

Do you know someone who embodies one or more of these survival skills? They probably don't see it in themselves. I believe this list represents many skills followers of Jesus can faithfully enact in our world. Imagine the inroads the church could have in these areas!

DISCUSS THIS

- What areas of your ministry make people feel most used? Which areas make people feel most utilized?
- How are you utilizing creativity among others to spur discipleship?
- Which friendships need to advance to partnerships? Which partnerships need to advance to collaboration?
- What are the greatest areas in which Christian unity has become a visible sign to your city?
- Where are trust, shared ownership, and co-creation present in your ministry? Where are they missing?
- Which of the six marks of a healthy team is most evident on your team?
- Which is least evident? How can you instill these as regular practices on your team?

CHAPTER 10

GO AHEAD AND FAIL

Finding our own voice may take the
greatest courage we've ever mustered.[1]
—Erwin McManus

Identity is the story we tell ourselves about
who we are and what the future holds for us.[2]
—Douglas Stone and Sheila Heen

Our imaginations are captured
poetically, not didactically. We're
hooked by stories, not bullet points.[3]
—James K. A. Smith

I was standing at the edge of the cliff looking down on the steaming reservoir forty feet below. My toes curled over the edge. I ducked under the branches ablaze with yellows, oranges, and reds. My adrenaline was pumping. I knew the water was deep enough. I just had to do it. I had only one simple decision to make. Gravity would take care of the rest. I hit harder than I had imagined. Ouch!

I awkwardly paddled to the bank, hiked back to the top, and got in line. There was guy on the ledge freaking out and blocking the launching pad. He wasn't making any progress. His fear had him caught in a vise.

"If you don't jump now, I guarantee it'll be harder in five minutes," I said to him. In all my years next to swimming holes, I have never seen someone wait thirty minutes and then jump. It doesn't work that way. When we don't check on the monster under the bed, it just keeps growing as it feeds on a steady diet of our insecurity. Don't wait for the perfect time to jump. By all means, check the water depth but go ahead—*jump*!

You can't avoid risk in life. No one gets a free pass from failure. If your narrative doesn't allow for failure, then your theology is brittle. We all have genius waiting to be unleashed, but risks help us realize it. Much of our genius is not tangible yet, but it is potential.[4] If I listed all my failures, this book would become several volumes. Creativity and failure are buddies. They hang out a lot.

This is where we circle back to the origin of genius we discussed in chapter 1. If our genius comes from us, the pressure is on. Our identity is on the line. Failure will be crushing. Each project is something to fear. But if the genius is from the Creator and is simply on loan to us, then the pressure is off. Failure is unavoidable, especially in creative endeavors. Our identity is secure. Our net worth doesn't determine our true worth. Because we *have* a genius instead of being a genius, we can neither take all the praise or criticism to heart.

From the Basement to the Gallery

Imagine you are an engineer by day and a painter by night. I know, weird combo. Every spare hour you have during the week you slip away to your basement to paint. Your painting stool feels like home.

When you smell the acrylic paint and pick up the brush, you feel like an angler next to a stream, a race car driver in a cockpit, a chef with a simmering skillet. Hours disappear as you clothe a stark-naked canvas with layers of popping color. Several times a month you complete a painting, stack it in a pile, and anxiously pull another blank canvas out of the plastic wrap.

One day your friends discover this stack of paintings in your basement. They are amazed. They convince you to finish a few more and get these into a local gallery for a show. After months of preparation, you hang the paintings on the gallery walls the night before the show. Once blank walls now frame explosions of paint, heart, and passion. Within minutes your giddy feelings about the show the next night have your heart racing and a sudden lump in your throat. You are terrified. *What if they don't get it? What if no one shows up? What if they don't like my style?*

Taking masterpieces from the basement to the gallery is one of the scariest things you will ever do. There is no wrong or right place or space to share your gifts, but you feel a driving sense to share them.

Sharing your gifts is a stewardship issue, but there is no template for how and where to offer these. It takes some wrestling. It's uncomfortable. It requires faith. You might risk more than you thought you could. Sharing a gift can feel completely unnatural. Publishing this book has been exciting, scary, and unnatural. Thoughts that have rattled around in my heart and spilled into conversations are compiled in a document, edited countless times, and priced for perfect strangers to buy. Weird, isn't it? We all feel these fears, but it's worth it.

From time to time we will be dismissed, laughed at, and misunderstood. Erwin McManus talked about the bipolar nature of creative risks: "We cannot live a life of passion and not know sorrow. To pursue a dream is to invite a nightmare! To live a life of love is to know betrayal and loss. The soul is both fragile and resilient."[5]

Fragility and resilience resonate deeply with me. I sense them both during the everyday daunting journey of faith. I feel them as a dad, husband, pastor, creative, friend, writer, and human. The challenge to remain resilient amid our fragility is a never-ending challenge.

Failure can propel us forward after it knocks us on our butts. It can actually create the space for beautiful things to grow in the future. Brené Brown refers to this as "composting your failure." Sometimes failure isn't brutal, it's subtle. It's the project that never went anywhere, the idea no one hated or loved, the concept no one at work ever wanted to help you with, or the side pursuit you never actually pursued. I've had a few small businesses that seemed to have momentum but never got beyond a cool idea.

There was a creative group at our church with big dreams. Artists know how to dream big, so there was no shortage of vision. There was a little momentum at first, but then they discovered limitations that squelched it from getting beyond a few experiments. It dissolved, and wasn't really talked about again. Some of those ladies stayed in contact. Years later they have formed an informal dance troupe that occasionally performs at women's prisons. I remember the disappointment in their eyes when this group allegedly failed. Maybe it was just a space for them to meet one another and scheme about future ministry opportunities with their craft. Don't write something off as a failure too soon. Our knowledge and vision are limited.

It's Worth It

Sheila was reserved and introverted and always sat in the back of the room. She never voluntarily shared information about herself. One day she lit up like I had never seen before. For more than ten years she had been writing, editing, rewriting, and re-editing a novel. She kept it tucked away from publishers. Eventually, and after much prodding from her husband, she realized it was time to bring her novel out of storage. She submitted the manuscript in a contest. She was petrified. But she walked home from that contest with first prize and a book contract. Her story grabbed the hearts of other readers. Her risk was worth it.

I was once a guitarist. I still dabble. Three chords have served me well over the years, but they have never done more than fill a coffee shop with loyal friends.

A few years ago I was helping to lead a retreat. God reminded me of a song that had spoken to me over the years about the topic we were covering at the retreat. The song haunted me. I had learned to play it more than ten years before and hadn't played it since.

After hearing the song on repeat in my head, I told the group, "I have a song to share with you guys." Finally I could sing this song, and it would stop driving me crazy. I belted the song with a lot of passion and a little skill. No one even acknowledged it afterward. Crickets.

In that moment I didn't think the risk was worth it. I filled in the blanks in my head: *It was terrible. It was a distraction. It didn't mean a thing to anyone. It wasn't worth the risk.* I was embarrassed and tempted to never pick up a guitar and play solo again.

Here's the good news: you *will* fail. You will fall short of your glorious expectations. You will be disappointed. That's when grace and identity become real.

Paul's words to the church at Corinth should comfort us:

> But he said to me, "My grace is sufficient for you, for my power is made perfect in weakness." Therefore I will boast all the more gladly of my weaknesses, so that the power of Christ may rest upon me. For the sake of Christ, then, I am content with weaknesses, insults, hardships, persecutions, and calamities. For when I am weak, then I am strong. (2 Cor. 12:9–10)

Desirable Difficulties

Our weaknesses and struggles remind us we are limited, human, and frail. We get frustrated and worn down. His mercies are new every morning even when the energy isn't. Our frailties help us remember we are not God. Paul frames these weaknesses as reasons to boast. Malcolm Gladwell framed these weaknesses as "desirable difficulties" in his book *David and Goliath*. Throughout the book, Gladwell tells stories of how successful leaders developed character and grit not just in spite of their weaknesses but *because* of their weaknesses.

Think about the flaws in our biblical heroes. Moses could lead people, but he was not an orator. His father-in-law, Jethro, had to give him leadership advice when he was heading toward burnout. Saul waged war against the church and was its greatest persecutor. God changed his name and made him the greatest strategist of the early church. He had a thorn in his flesh, a weakness that kept him humble. The one who once persecuted the church led many to faith, and wrote half the New Testament. David, "a man after God's own heart," committed adultery and conceived a murder plot to cover it up. Scandalous!

Many of our views of successful and strong leadership are more cultural than they are biblical. American culture worships entrepreneurship, success, and innovation. Everyone seems to want to start something from scratch and be their own boss. We are obsessed with the question *"Will it work?"* We love the idea of risk, but at our core, we want full assurance that the plane is going to fly, the idea is going to stick, the event is going to be epic, and the business is going to make it. By its very nature, risks live in the land of uncertainty.

It's About Obedience, Not Success

Instead of "Will it work?" we must learn to ask, "Should I try it?" We avoid risk today at all costs and worship safety and security. In her book *Daring Greatly*, Brené Brown repeatedly posed the question, "What is worth doing even if you fail?"[6] I try to ask myself this question every month.

The church is heading into unmapped territory. Every day, every week, every season is pregnant with risk and possibility. When we wade into the rapids of risk, we find ourselves immersed in the current of faith. God can handle more than we throw at Him.

Our culture is also heading into unmapped territory. Technology too. There is a lot we don't know, and this has bred a culture of fear. This is the time for a courageous church, not a fearful church.

Our goal is not success but obedience. We must learn to

celebrate obedience in those around us. God never asks us to be successful; He asks us to be faithful. The gospel doesn't promise us surety; it invites us to risk. As leaders, we must celebrate risk and normalize the perceived failures of those around us.

> Share things that didn't work out great for you.
> Share things that didn't work out as you had imagined for your church.
> Share how you have been disappointed in the past.
> But please, share that you and others were obedient to the voice of our Father.

Our church website includes a section about a dark season in our past when we took inordinate risks that ended poorly. That season doesn't define us, and we don't need to hide it. It's part of our story, and our story isn't finished. Without a culture of risk in your church or organization, you can't push into the unknown.

There Is Grace and Space to Fail

When I began inviting people into apprenticeships many years ago, I saw something curious in young leaders. They yearned for a space to try things that seemed a little crazy. They had ideas that kept them up at night, they shared them around campfires, and they studied them in classrooms. They wanted space to experiment, but they were also terrified of failure. Somewhere deep in their minds, they thought, *If I fail at something during my first church ministry experience, I will never succeed long term in ministry.*

At the apprenticeship orientation, I told them: "This is a safe space to fail. If you don't fail at anything during this time, you aren't taking risks."

I set the bar both high and low. A few of their ideas were brilliant and others didn't work out. I have found the same thing to be true for me and the ministries I have led.

The Free-Throw Line vs. the Batter's Box

I grew up playing basketball and baseball. Most of my afternoons and evenings were spent either on the court or on the diamond. In basketball, free throws are considered free points. Some players make close to 90 percent of their free throws. But when a player misses a free throw at the end of the game, a lot of criticism is directed at the missed free throw and the scrub who missed it.

Stepping to the plate in baseball is a completely different situation. At .366 over twenty-six seasons, Ty Cobb has the best lifetime batting average ever recorded in the major leagues. But this means he failed more than six out of ten times at the plate. And he was the best. Most good baseball players hit around .250. We get used to baseball players failing at home plate, but we are disgusted when basketball players fail at the free-throw line.

We live a faith-filled life at home plate, not at the free-throw line. The best season I had at home plate, I felt the most freedom to fail. I was young, expectations were low, I batted high in the lineup, and I swung by instinct. I attacked the ball because I didn't think about strikeouts. I had nothing to lose.

You will succeed at some tasks and fail at many. Go out there, swing the bat, and don't think about striking out.

Creativity rarely rises out of environments where failure is shamed. Where there is space to move and try and fail, there is experimentation. Ed Catmull observed: "From a very early age, the message is drilled into our heads: Failure is bad; failure means you didn't study or prepare; failure means you slacked off or—worse!—aren't smart enough to begin with. Thus, failure is something to be ashamed of."[7]

Often, as kingdom leaders, we feel we must be strong and avoid failure. This couldn't be further from the truth, but it sounds familiar to all of us. I highly recommend my brother J. R.'s book, *Fail: Finding Hope and Grace in the Midst of Ministry Failure.* Business leaders, entrepreneurs, and real estate agents are also terrified to fail. Fear of failure isn't a church thing; it's a human thing.

I remember a risk I took as the leader of a large gathering. It was awesome in my head. I recruited two other leaders to gather a group around them to process what they were learning. It sounded like a processing exercise they would do at Apple or Google sitting on a yoga ball. Not only did it fail, everyone felt painfully awkward while it was going on. It felt like my first middle school dance. The leaders dismissed the session early to give it a proper death.

I've learned to start with "let's give it a shot" instead of "this is going to be great." Perhaps the greatest thing you can embed in a leadership culture is an obvious *freedom to fail.* And the church leadership should model this for the whole organization. What does it say if every program you attempt succeeds wildly? If your organization has always been on the ascent, this can be dangerous and breed a fear of empire toppling. People learn to extend grace to their leaders if it has been modeled for them. At some point, you are going to have to stand up and say, "I made a mistake. I thought it would work," "I didn't see that happening," "I'm not perfect," or "I'm so sorry."

Every act of creativity is a risk, some just feel bigger than others.

Every act of obedience takes faith, some are just scarier than others.

Are you humble enough to admit when something doesn't work? I watch leaders painfully hold on to their pride when everyone knows the idea didn't work. The only true failure is failing to admit you failed. "Let's give it a shot" often leads to "well, *that* didn't work."

You will only develop a culture of risky kingdom living if people feel the freedom to fail. When people feel secure, half-formed ideas develop into faith risks and people will experiment outside of their comfort zones. You can challenge those around you only to the level they feel safe. A church with a culture of love and risk sends people out beyond its walls to love and risk in their community. Just *doing* church isn't a risk, but *impacting* communities requires a culture of risk taking.

I'm not an advocate for doing things poorly. Excellence matters, but faith matters more. Calculate your risks, do as well as you can with the resources you've been given, but obey when the Father speaks. We have no idea how our faith risks will end, but they are worth doing even if we fail.

The Power of Unlikely Partnership

Kim and her family have been part of our church for a long time. She and her husband, Rick, own a boutique in a business district, and she has a lot of street cred. They are great folks who work hard and have created a fun culture in their shop. They know the heartbreak of bad business months and the beauty of watching someone light up when they find the right dress or gift for a friend. I love the artsy culture in this shop, but truth be told, I feel pretty creepy walking around a women's boutique. I get weird glances from the women browsing in the shop.

Just after releasing my first book, *Staying Is the New Going*, Kim came up to me with a gleam in her eye. She wanted to sell my book in her shop. I would never have thought about this partnership, but I immediately loved the idea. After all, a book about localizing and loving where God has placed us should be on real shelves in a real shop in our community instead of just on Amazon. Kim bought a pile of books and put them in her shop. This was the only Jesus-ish item in the shop. Kim took the tangible risk to put a Christian product in her shop.

Next time I saw Kim, she said, "I have had more conversations about Jesus in five days in the shop than I had in the last year!" Kim keeps ordering books and selling them or giving them away as she seeds Jesus into conversations. I am so proud of Kim and Rick. They are being obedient. It gives me great joy to partner with Kim in her ministry to women in our city. I never would have thought to ask her to sell my book in her shop, and I never would have guessed how God would use a little bit of conversation to let Kim dig into the lives of other women. Kim is a missionary who happens to run a women's boutique.

We need stories like this rising out of people in our churches. If you aren't embracing a culture of risk, you won't multiply leaders who are taking risks. The very act of discipleship, leadership development, and sending leaders are risks.

The Faith-Full Experiment

Innovation is alluring. Everyone seems to want to be an innovator these days. We don't often consider the interconnection between innovation and failure. Innovation only exists when failure is not only possible but probable. Every human fears failure. The ones who form the vanguard are the ones who keep taking risks when they know what they're doing might not work out. There is great fear in the heart of an artist before receiving critique. The process leaves the artist feeling vulnerable as they wait for a response.

We wonder if others will understand our work or understand us. Some of my favorite artists, musicians, and movement makers started with ideas, riffs, and mediums I didn't resonate with at first. Over time I have fallen in love with their work. They were acquired tastes.

Failure gets in the way for all of us, but there is no way around it. In the words of one of my favorite children's books: "We can't go over it, we can't go under it. Oh no! We have to go through it."[8]

Facing failure head-on is a faith-full exercise. Experimentation has everything to do with our theology.

Faith is based on trust.

Innovation creates something new and makes it see-able to others.

If we believe creativity is God-given, we must use it. God is not preoccupied with our performance. The result matters far less than the faith we muster to try something. When we care more about God's validation than acceptance by others, people can exit the gallery of our lives booing and laughing and we can still hold our heads high.

Fear of failure is the absence of freedom. Perhaps you feel

like you possess a lesser gift, one that won't be celebrated in arenas, at church gatherings, and in the public square. The thought of truly exercising your creativity might feel scary or mundane or frustrating or too big of a risk.

But God has gifted and wired each of us to do something unique, and there is freedom at the end of that road. We are deeply loved sons and daughters, not clients and performers.

DISCUSS THIS

- What failures have propelled you into victories?
- How has failure been treated in the environments you've been part of?
- What is worth you doing even if you fail at it?
- What are some tangible ways you are giving others around you the freedom to fail?
- What risks do you need to take in the next month?
- What is the true fear lurking beneath your fear of failure?

CHAPTER 11

HOW TO SEND A GENIUS WELL

Passion is the fuel of life. It is the
great source of energy and drive.
—Bob Buford

For we are not, like so many, peddlers of God's
word, but as men of sincerity, as commissioned
by God, in the sight of God we speak in Christ.
—2 Corinthians 2:17

The more we get what we now call "ourselves"
out of the way and let him take us over,
the more truly ourselves we become.
—C. S. Lewis

Bruce is the best networker I know. He connects people so they can accomplish more together. He's done this many times for me. When he was in his late twenties, two friends helped him recognize this gift of connecting people he had practiced so naturally since middle school. They helped him look back and connect the dots of his wiring. They helped him see his gift was something God could use. This realization put rocket boosters on his relationships and his career.

Bruce shared an idea he was passionate about with a mentor. That man connected him with three others who would resonate with his idea. One of those leaders connected deeply with it and opened the door for Bruce to share it with others. The seed sprouted, put down roots, and over many years, it has multiplied to thousands of leaders worldwide. It has led to books, films, and leaders from every sector of society having their foundations shaken.[1] Today, Bruce points back to one moment, one man, one referral, as the tipping point for thousands of lives.

Bruce is always searching for the tipping point[2] for others that might be one connection away. He loves to create moments when two people can help an idea thrive. He doesn't do this for his own gain; he loves the feeling of connecting two people to accomplish something amazing. He gets to experience the pure joy of seeing the kingdom advance. He leverages the power of introduction.

Through constant advances in communication technology, connecting people happens faster today than ever before. There is so much kingdom potential when we connect leaders. The Holy Spirit is the master networker, connecting people and communities to experience the Father's love. These introductions leave traces into eternity. The gift of meaningful referrals isn't listed among the spiritual gifts in Scripture, but it can be deeply fruitful in kingdom work.

God has unlocked heaps of kingdom impact through Bruce's referrals. A few men took the time to affirm how God had wired Bruce and validated his gift. They unleashed him to live his God-given genius for connecting people for the sake of the world.

Recovering Our Imagination

Eugene Peterson is an inspiration to masses of leaders today. Millions have been impacted by the fresh language in his paraphrase, *The Message*. That includes Bono. So many of us want to go the distance in a world of chronic burnout. When asked, "What gives you hope for the church today?" Peterson answered, "Those in ministry are recovering a pastoral imagination." For a time, it seems, pastors misplaced the ability to draw outside the lines, to create something different than they had seen before. Perhaps we are thawing out and slowly regaining our imagination again. People are not products. Churches are not businesses. Souls are not prizes.

Ministers of the gospel, paid and unpaid, are taking risks to be exactly who God has made them to be. No, this doesn't always end well, but we can't afford to not live as God intends us to live. Authenticity breeds more authenticity. When someone shares a raw or self-deprecating answer to a question, you feel invited to do the same. When you share a failure story, someone else feels they can do the same. Authenticity is a gift you offer and a practice you model. Church leaders, when you offer this gift, your leadership team and congregation will eventually respond. It will likely function as an invitation for them to do likewise.

It can feel much riskier to offer up our gifts outside the walls of the church. We lose some predictability. We can no longer rely on a map.

I met with an evangelist who shared stories of gang members coming to know Jesus and families becoming whole again. He also shared about having a loaded gun pressed against his head.

Paul offered his gift to the Gentiles, leaving the subculture of life and ministry he was acquainted with. Titles and the education he had collected meant next to nothing to the Gentiles. But I believe focusing on a new group and a new subculture actually made Paul come alive. Paul's and Peter's lives only made sense outside the walls of the church. They didn't throw out the traditions, but they embraced the risk of exiting their comfort zones.

The same is true for us. When we exit the safer confines of our church programs, we find ourselves rediscovering faith. We feel a mixture of terrified and excited at what lies ahead. It's "terriciting."[3]

Uncovering and Releasing Genius

Remember, your genius is given by God, confirmed in community, and aimed at kingdom impact. Here are four crucial actions to help release the genius in others:

- Tell others they have a genius and God crafted them uniquely.
- Begin observing and affirming their genius.
- Remind them their gifts should be aimed at kingdom work.
- Suggest practical opportunities to exercise their genius for the sake of the world.

Jim Collins wrote the groundbreaking book *Good to Great* that sold millions of copies. Perhaps the most earth-shattering finding is that people want to follow competent servant leaders and hate being led by prideful, controlling leaders. It turns out the best research confirms that leading in Jesus' way is actually the best way to lead.

The best leaders I know are willing to clear out of the way, because the work isn't about them. The most intelligent individuals don't feel the need to be the smartest but to draw out the smarts and creativity of others.[4] We have become obsessed with being innovative leaders. We need to find other innovators around us and help match them with opportunities. God has created geniuses; we just need to uncover where genius is hiding in others. God makes creative geniuses, but we affirm and launch them.

A church with a sending culture is a church that believes God creates masterpieces. Sending churches don't believe they own people, but they are spiritual caretakers and equippers of a congregation. When we send leaders we help usher them into the next steps of life and ministry. Don't get me wrong, it hurts to let them go. A sending church deeply invests in people, apprenticing them for greatness, and is willing to let them go when it's time. Sending leaders are selfless, faithful leaders who trust God.

Whenever we send a leader from our church, I peek during prayer to see hands raised, teary eyes, and people who have been deeply impacted by these folks. It hurts the flesh, but it refreshes the soul. What feels like a loss for your church is a win for the kingdom.

Creating New Metrics

I love to fish—usually. Once I had kids old enough to sit beside the water's edge, I imagined peacefully fly-fishing while my kids quietly admired their dad. Picture the iconic film *A River Runs*

Through it. Thirty seconds after unloading the car, they were throwing rocks in the water and yelling across the lake. I became the fishing librarian, telling the kids to quiet down, stop yelling, and focus on the task at hand. Cranky dad took over. Not exactly what I pictured.

My mind-set determines how much fishing will happen that day. I have shifted my fishing expectations these days. At the beginning of the day I determine if the day is about just having fun with my kids or landing trout. Is this a catch-and-release day or am I going to have fish tacos for dinner? Do I need to put down the fishing rod, skip rocks with my kids and scare away every fish in the lake? The joy of the rest of my day will be determined by my answers.

Metrics matter. They tell us what we're aiming at. The aims of our church will determine much of our joy and emotions as we do ministry. We should be far more excited about releasing people into obedience than corralling them into pews. Please hear me: involvement in a local church body matters! We love to have people in our church gatherings, but what are we doing with them after that? Those people can launch into every niche, industry, sphere, and neighborhood in our city with the message of Jesus in their bones.

I hope you are longing for a kingdom vision to rise out of your church and into your community. But you've got work to do. The output won't change until you change what you value. Americans are calculated people. We have goals and we are focused (more like obsessed) with reaching them. If we want our results to change, our metrics will also have to change.

People often say, "Don't measure results, it's unspiritual." That's bogus. We are going to measure things; it's ingrained in us. It isn't unspiritual to measure things. We just need to make sure to measure the right things. You will need to sit down as a leadership team and form a robust list of new metrics if you want to see your people released into the community.

Reggie McNeal has suggested the following metrics for leaders and churches:[5]

- Number of growing relationships with people who are not Jesus followers
- Number of personal relationships with community leaders
- Number of venues for international personal service in the community
- Number of hours or venues of personal service in the local community
- Number of stories of external missional experiences used in your speaking

Be creative and come up with some new metrics that fit your church. A friend carefully measures the percentage of his time dedicated to discipling others. Each year he hopes to make a little more money in his business so he can spend a little less time selling things and more time focusing on discipling people. He logs his time in an app on his phone. I love this.

Second, make sure you model these at the staff level of your church. For example, our church staff is encouraged to spend several days per year helping other churches or organizations. This models that we are *for* others in their kingdom work and we want to help. Our senior pastor also did the legwork to start a network of pastors who gather regularly in our city. This has set an expectation for the staff that some of their time each month should be spent building the church in our city.

This is a great use of time, although it can feel selfish to develop friendships with other ministry leaders who won't help the bottom line of discipleship within our church. When people see you modeling what matters to your church and your community, they feel they have permission to do this too. In our last teaching team meeting, we shared how God was at work around and through us with friends who are far from the church. This leaks into our preaching and teaching. As the adage goes, "Leadership leads, but it also leaks." Make space for the things you want your church to start doing and keep doing.

The Church As a Sending Center

A friend runs a local café and gastropub. This is a great place for business leaders, foodies, coffee fiends, and craft-beer advocates to hang out and meet people. While the food and drinks are well curated and locally sourced, the most impressive thing about this place is how the management treats their employees. My friend wants to see his employees succeed, and he realizes they have a shelf life. Even the best ones.

He has had several hard conversations with his employees. Many of these revolve around challenging them to pursue their future dreams. Yes, this involves exiting the staff to head somewhere else. It is hard to send out your best employees, especially when they have been there for a long time and are very proficient. He chooses instead to see God's vision for their lives and their future instead of trying to hoard employees.

This is how we should function. We can become a genius launch pad, organizing and deploying people into the next step of their journeys.

The church in Antioch is my favorite example of a sending church:

> Now there were in the church at Antioch prophets and teachers, Barnabas, Simeon who was called Niger, Lucius of Cyrene, Manaen a lifelong friend of Herod the tetrarch, and Saul. While they were worshiping the Lord and fasting, the Holy Spirit said, "Set apart for me Barnabas and Saul for the work to which I have called them." Then after fasting and praying they laid their hands on them and sent them off. (Acts 13:1–3)

Look at what we see here:

They Had a Diverse Ministry Team

What an incredible gathering of men who formed this strong ministry team at Antioch. The hub of the church had shifted from Jerusalem to Antioch. It was a leadership development lab and hub. They had amazing leadership resources there.

It Became a Sending Center

They took it seriously. Sending affects your church, families, and the communities where those leaders land. They worshiped, fasted, and when the Spirit spoke, they obeyed. It was time for Barnabas and Saul (Paul) to go. It's as if they had too much talent in one place and God needed to spread the love to other places.

They Laid Hands on Them and Sent Them

The laying on of hands is a uniquely powerful experience. We do this regularly at our church. How can something so biblical hurt so badly? Our church is committed to sending our best.

The reality is that God sends them by putting desires for a new place, a new task, or new people in their hearts; we simply acknowledge it. When a team of people gathers and lays hands on their leaders, they are expressing a few things:

We see God at work in you. We have observed God working in and through you. We affirm that.

We are for you even though we won't be with you. Some in the congregation will hold their hands up symbolically while a group gathers and physically lays their hands on them. They go on behalf of a church family, but they are still part of our extended family.

God's presence is with you. A group of people around you is a physical representation of the love and power of God. John 14 reminds us: "I will ask the Father, and he will give you another Helper [think comforter, advocate, counselor], to be with you forever, even the Spirit of truth, whom the world cannot receive, because it neither sees him nor knows him. You know him, for he dwells with you and will be in you" (vv. 16–17).

It's easy to think commissioning is just an expression of the early church. We also see it in the Old Testament, particularly in the book of Numbers:

The LORD said to Moses, "Take Joshua the son of Nun, a man in whom is the Spirit, and lay your hand on him. Make him stand before Eleazar the priest and all the congregation, and you shall commission him in their sight. *You shall invest him with some of your authority, that all the congregation of the people of Israel may obey.* And he shall stand before Eleazar the priest, who shall inquire for him by the judgment of the Urim before the LORD. At his word they shall go out, and at his word they shall come in, both he and all the people of Israel with him, the whole congregation." And Moses did as the LORD commanded him. He took Joshua and made him stand before Eleazar the priest and the whole congregation, and he laid his hands on him and commissioned him as the LORD directed through Moses. (27:18–23)

What a beautiful picture of listening to God and investing authority in a younger leader (verse 20, italicized above). This is a picture of a God-inspired succession plan. Moses is investing some of his authority in Joshua. Who are you investing with some of your authority? Who are you taking risks with? Who are you giving your best time and influence to?

In Deuteronomy, we see the succession plan come to completion: "And the LORD commissioned Joshua the son of Nun and said, 'Be strong and courageous, for you shall bring the people of Israel into the land that I swore to give them. I will be with you'" (31:23).

Moses saw the land, but Joshua would lead Israel into it. God has tasks picked out for leaders. Although Moses didn't accompany Joshua into the promised land, his leadership and authority went with him. Joshua had watched him lead, and God used Moses to bless Joshua and Joshua to bless Israel. Sometimes God gives you a dream that someone else is supposed to accomplish.

God Isn't a Bouncer

Church ministry can be ironic. When we dedicate ourselves to becoming saint equippers, we will begin to raise up others around us who are gifted. Eventually we might find a really solid team around us. God isn't a bouncer who likes to break up parties, but He moves people on when it is time.

Our church lamented how it seems like we are sending out another couple every other week. But God has been more than backfilling our team with other leaders. I don't understand kingdom math, but we've watched God do it consistently. Other churches and leaders will benefit from the leaders we raise up, but ultimately God's kingdom benefits.

Sometimes what seems like a call to go to another place might just be a desire. We are infatuated with the future. This infatuation leads us to fantasies of landing in other places with new assignments among different people groups. Many times we are just bored with where we are living, the season we are currently in, and the people we are currently around. After seeing these desires in myself and countless leaders around me, we began to name it. This wrestling caused my family to grow deeper roots in our city and neighborhood. I explain this at length in my book *Staying Is the New Going: Choosing to Love Where God Places You.*

When leaders come to me and excitedly share about the call of God on their life into a new season, place, or assignment, I have learned to listen, pray for them, and ask them some hard questions. As leaders, equippers, and mentors, we can partner to help others discern whether God is moving them to another place or simply asking them to press in deeper right where they are.

Most churches don't give their leaders a kickoff, they punt

them. Sometimes they slip out the door without receiving the blessing of being sent by a church body. They miss out on blessing and so does the church!

God blesses the generosity of churches who send leaders out. Another church might be gathered at the very same moment to send leaders who are coming your way. Some church leaders allow jealousy and woundedness to arise in these moments. That leads to all kinds of ugly feelings: insecurity, betrayal, and mistrust. I have heard countless stories of the sending process being derailed as deep wounds develop at the hands of an insecure leader. They withhold their blessing from a leader who is following God into the great unknown.

I realize this goes both ways: many leaders don't know how to exit well and launch into a new season. We need to put extra care into how we send our leaders out. I have been privileged to see many situations where this has been done well. In the last year I have worked closely with two church plants where established churches have chosen to send well and release leaders to go with them. In turn, these young leaders feel connected to an established congregation that can support them in various ways. The established congregation gets to be part of those who are leaving a robust, living legacy in their own city. It's a beautiful thing.

Sending: It Hurts So Good

Even in the perfect situation, sending is painful. Human hearts aren't meant to disconnect, but pain and blessing often go together. Think about childbirth and adoption. One thing to remember is that most times you don't have a choice. Rarely can people be convinced to stay.

I have committed to help people discern their next step but to never try to detain someone from God's next assignment. Even when it doesn't sound wise, God reminds me He's taking care of them.

We are a church-planting church. We pray over trusted church planters, and we give an open fishing license to join them. I want to be part of a church that has dreams the size of the kingdom, not the size of our congregation.

As you read this, you may be thinking, *That sounds great, but if we did this, our whole church would leave. How do you keep anyone around to develop children, lead the music, or build ministry teams?*

Every pastor feels some fear about this, and lead pastors feel this the most. Let me assure you that I feel the same things. It's human. Sending is an act of faith. It's not natural to develop leaders and willingly let go of them. Not only are they competent, but they are the fruit of your labor! Fears will haunt you, and you will think about the impact they could have if they stayed or the position they might fill in a year from now. You will convince yourself why they simply must stay.

After every sending prayer we've done, I see tears. We inherently know this is kingdom stuff. It's transcendent. We are doing something bigger than us. It not only feels right, but it's obedience. I fear the day when someone says, "I was trying to obey God and you got in the way!"

The Future of the Church

Commissioning and sending leaders always gets me excited for the future of the church. Younger leaders are stepping into bigger spaces of influence. They won't look, talk, or make decisions like the leaders who came before them, but that doesn't mean they aren't godly leaders.

Older leaders, who can you lay your hands on and lend some of your authority to? Who carries the spiritual DNA of your church? Who can you give spiritual confidence to?

Commissioning is not a sign a leader is perfect or complete. It's a sign they are set apart and affirmed.

The laying on of hands was a pathway for God to empower Timothy, a young leader who likely grew up without a father. God chose to give Timothy a powerful kingdom gift through spiritual fathers:

> Do not neglect the gift you have, which was given you by prophecy when the council of elders laid their hands on you. Practice these things, immerse yourself in them, so that all may see your progress. (1 Tim. 4:14–15)

One of my favorite leadership development processes ends with commissioning. The process looks like this:

- The leader shares one or two paradigm-shifting things God has revealed to them through the learning and community during the year.
- The rest of us share the growth we have observed in them. They are always surprised by some of these. They are too close to themselves to see their unique genius.
- We lay hands on them and pray for them. We pray about their universal call to make disciples and the unique call God is revealing to them.
- We wrestle through how to do this in a biblical, affirming,

and healthy way that is full of grace and truth. There are certainly times not to commission leaders, but many are waiting to be released. I think we are more in danger of withholding commissioning than giving it too liberally.

- Release people to be reminded of the original commissioning: the Great Commission. In Matthew 28:18 we are reminded that "all authority in heaven and on earth" had been given to Jesus, and He transferred that authority to the disciples and to every disciple after that moment. Often commissioning is simply a reminder of Matthew 28 and the charge to make disciples of all nations.

A Quick Note About Ordination

Ordination and commissioning are slightly different, but both should come from a careful watch of what God is doing in a leader's life.

Ordination can be a tricky thing. Churches and denominations all seem to do this differently. I work with a lot of different denominations and tribes, so I am learning all the nuances. I'm okay with different ordination processes, but let's acknowledge this can be confusing. Some are required to read large amounts of material, write dissertation-like papers, and come before a local or denominational board. Others are simply prayed for with their elders. Others are observed closely for a season of ministry, a probation period of sorts, and then released with full authority as a pastor in that church.

Be careful not to liken ordination to a hoop to jump through. It's sometimes just a detail done for tax purposes for the IRS so folks can get the benefits of being considered clergy. No, it's not a mail-order collar, but (strangely) it also has tax benefits. Spiritual ordination should never be confused with tax deductions. I believe it's fine for spiritual leaders (clergy) to receive this designation, but we need to create different tracks for *legal* benefits and *spiritual* ordination.

At our church we have decided to have our pastoral team and elders identify the fruit in their lives, watching them faithfully serve behind the scenes and shepherd the flock with care. After a period of time we bring them before our pastoral team and elders, lay hands on them, affirm their obedience, and pray over them. This is one of the biggest blessings you can give to pastors, especially young ones.

The Sending

At Vanguard Church we end each service with a sending. It wasn't always this way. We used to conclude our services with an awkward mix between "Peace out y'all," "See you next week," "Go Broncos!" and "Oops, I forgot to announce—." Our worship pastor prayed, thought, and dreamed about how we might send people out each week in a courageous way. When he shared the rough draft with me, I knew it was going to change our church. And it absolutely has.

Before a baptism, I love to hear a person's story of transformation and their understanding of their sent-ness. They have been invited to join God's mission, and they have accepted the invitation.

It's permission, a reminder of release back into the same

world, neighborhood, job, and relationships. It's a living liturgy. It's a reminder to obey, even if we fail. It's a closing that's actually an opening. We have a genius, the great Genius Maker. We are also geniuses, because we are created in His image. Both are true. Both matter.

I want to leave you with a blessing in the form of a challenge. Imagine this book was a gathering of sorts. Before slamming this book closed and leaving the room, we look around and wait for a signal to grab our things. Hold on! Before we grab our bags, I want to send you with something to chew on and something to live by.

The Sending

God, You are my Father, and I will follow You
I am chosen, forgiven, redeemed, and restored
I am broken and mending and called by the Lord
I'm a leader, a multiplier
I'll pray and I'll love
As I live as a steward of what God has done
I'll worship King Jesus in spirit and truth
And give every day God as praise just to You
So here I am, Lord, in response to Your call
Send me and spend me I give You my all
God, You are our Father, and we will follow You.[6]

DISCUSS THIS

- How are you practicing authenticity? What have the results been?
- What are your fears in sending leaders who God has called elsewhere?
- Who can you lay your hands on and lend some of your authority to? Who can you give spiritual confidence to?
- In which areas can you exercise faith by affirming and releasing leaders into their next assignment?
- What practices can your ministry develop to send leaders?

EPILOGUE

The same phrase is repeated to each of the seven churches in the book of Revelation: "He who has an ear, let him hear what the Spirit says to the churches."[1] I pray you would tune the hearing aid of your heart to the frequency of God's whispers.

Perhaps you are listening for whispers as you feel underwhelmed by your current impact.

Perhaps you are listening on behalf of your church, feeling like you are the captain of a ship with no crew. You are yearning for God to use you to raise up leaders around you.

Perhaps you feel your tribe has been leashed for too long. You and your friends are bored because you don't feel invited into a deeper narrative.

Perhaps one nugget stuck out to you from this book and you'll forget everything else you've read.

I pray your ears have heard and your actions will follow. I hope God uses this book to unlock something in you, your tribe, and your congregation that has been locked for a while.

God uses listeners to shape churches and communities. Keep listening to the whispers of the Holy Spirit. Each of the seven churches in Revelation had unique strengths, weaknesses, and issues. There was struggle, drama, distraction, and victory.

The same is true of us. There is no easy map I can give you to understand who God has made you to be. I only hope to remind you that you are unique and you are gifted. So are those around you. Keep creating. Keep risking. Keep showing up. Press on, geniuses!

I'd love to hear how this book affected you. Drop me a line at Alan@stayforth.com.

ACKNOWLEDGMENTS

My bride, Julie, for your prayers, encouragement, and wisecracks along the way.

Greg Ligon and Mark Sweeney for believing in this idea.

J. R. for your thoughts along the way.

Mom for your sustaining prayer.

Starving kingdom artists who feel alone and unaffirmed. Keep quietly creating things, teams, ideas, and messes.

Mike Hamel for your constant inspiration to hone my craft.

Leadership Network for your years of believing in the church and helping to spark change.

Mary Hollingsworth, LeeEric Fesko, and the whole Thomas Nelson team for chipping away at this message and making it look dapper.

The geniuses I interviewed in the book: Bruce McNicol, Dan Ewing, Bryson Foster, Simon Scionka, Myron Pierce, Ron Dotzler, Kim and Rick McKenna, Chuck McKenzie, John and Sue Cressman, Mike Worley Jr., and Etienne Hardre. Your stories brought flesh, bones, and sinew to this message.

The team at Vanguard Church for your encouragement and challenge. Doing team with you has been really stretching and really fun.

SLIM SUMMARY

You're short on time. You're in the middle of reading six books, but you wanted to crack this one open. You promised your team you would have it read by Tuesday, and it's Monday night. You've come to the right place.

This is a brief overview of *Everyone's a Genius*. My hope is this can help you retain the content, teach it to others, and share it, tweet it, and pass it along to others. #everyonesagenius

Chapter 1: Where Does Genius Come From?

- The Greeks caged creativity as the *daemon* and the Romans as the *genius*. They believed you *had* a genius.
- Everyone is a genius; actually everyone *has* a genius, namely, the almighty God.
- Your genius is given by God, confirmed in community, and aimed at kingdom impact.
- Most people sitting in church pews don't sense they are part of God's great mission to redeem all things.
- When we believe we are the source of creativity, we get all the credit and all the pressure. When we realize creativity is inspired by God, He can get the worship.

- Creativity is both nature and nurture; God gives us gifts and we develop them.
- Time, hard work, and the voices of others will help us to grow into the kind of leaders God has created us to be.
- The blessing of God isn't just for us. Great artists understand their art isn't just for them; it's a gift to be shared.
- One day God will hold us accountable for what we did with the talent He gave us.
- God has given each of us unique tools to retell the gospel narrative in tangible and attractive ways.
- There is no template for how our genius can creatively tell the kingdom story, but there certainly is a calling.

Chapter 2: What Counts?

- Every mission-minded follower of Jesus asks the question, "What counts as ministry?"
- Many people believe ministry is reserved for those with the title of pastor and church leaders who talk from a stage or lead Bible studies.
- We crave originality and authenticity, yet we find ourselves copying others in style, language, rituals, food, and relationships.
- We are all completely normal yet completely original.
- Church leaders have inadvertently put the creativity of their congregations on a leash. This leaves people feeling safe but not fulfilled.
- When we unleash others, we show we trust them.

- A leashed congregation may be easier to lead and control, but that obsession with safety will lead a church on a journey to a slow, safe death.
- Every church needs to create a new grid to more effectively celebrate, develop, and send people to inhabit and impact our world.
- *The credibility gap:* people are suspicious of followers of Jesus because they believe we only want to convert them.
- *The validation gap:* church leaders are failing to recognize, equip, and release leaders to make an impact on our world.
- The church is leaking creativity. It is a slow drip resulting in a loss of creative pressure.
- Diversity of talent should not drive us to compare ourselves to others but to admire and affirm others. Every one of us is a valid and valuable part of God's plan to restore all things.
- When people find out what counts in an environment, they start doing it.
- *Peer-desire cultures* envy genius and diminish it, but *empowerment cultures* celebrate the diversity of genius.
- Our world is becoming more diverse in the creativity we honor. This makes it even more crucial for the church to expand its view of genius.

Chapter 3: Creative Espionage

- Humans aren't props or propagators; we are creative, valuable beings.

- One role of Jesus' followers is to dig below the surface to find value in others, because we are all created in God's image.
- Followers of Jesus must become genius spies who affirm and fan creatives into life.
- We should constantly be following the trail of creativity in others and affirming what we find in them.
- A mature body of Christ will impact families, neighborhoods, cities, and the world. Churches mature as they take responsibility for recognizing and equipping others.
- The true work of ministry is not found in developing our gifts, but in developing the gifts of those around us.
- *Falsely humble leadership culture* fails to recognize, raise up, and multiply leaders out of an overreaction to pride.
- *Prideful leadership culture* yields pressure to produce and be validated out of an obsession with excellence.
- *Empowering leadership culture* finds a balance between false humility and pride, yielding freedom to take risks and exercise gifts. It affirms God's role as *the* Creator and the *imago dei* embedded in every human being.
- Everyone who is part of God's family has the authority of the Father. Through the Great Commission, Jesus gives us authority to do ministry.
- Study those around you. What people naturally get excited about says a lot about them.
- If we want to reach people no one else is reaching, we must mobilize different types of people and validate different ways to reach people.
- The church should be the greatest crowdsourcing engine on the planet.

- Every human being needs validation. We all long to know we are valuable, our work is valid, and we are worth celebrating.
- What people are celebrated for, positively or negatively, will be stamped on their souls.
- The people of Jesus should become masters at helping others discover who they are, what they are gifted at, and how this can bless the world.

Chapter 4: The New Geniuses

- Authenticity is crucial to both creativity and ministry.
- Hospitality is important. Having an open life will take work and sacrifice, but it sets the table for conversation, prayer, and dreams.
- Liturgy is important. The statements we repeat and the rhythms we complete ready us for reentry into God's kingdom work.
- Creation is not self-induced; it is a divine breeze blowing through us. We have the spirit of God running through our veins, bringing us joy in the privilege that we *get* to serve God.
- Artists are all around you, though you might not see them. They are subtly making beauty, telling truth, and creating subversive movements.
- This chapter includes a list of eighteen types of creators we commonly overlook in our culture. Take time to browse and then make a list of those folks around you who represent these areas.

- We need people who will thoughtfully engage in areas and causes the gospel beckons us to talk about, preach about, act on, and advocate for.

Chapter 5: Genius Is a Process

- We often seek God for an answer when He wants to teach us a process. We want a box checked, but He wants to dive below the surface.
- Genius is given by God, but it is honed through processes. It takes discipline to continue to create over an extended time.
- Most great ideas emerge from a process.
- I have yet to meet anyone who regularly takes on big projects and doesn't have a process.
- If you want to produce more, you will have to be content with doing less.
- We live in a world that wants final-draft excellence with first-draft effort. You can't escape rough drafts in the creative process.
- Wading through criticism is one of the hardest, most humbling things you can do. Give criticism gently and receive it readily.
- Be careful labeling others "prodigy" and yourself "late bloomer."
- The creative process grows our stewardship, lessens our envy, and evens our expectations.
- We crave significance so much that we want to be known and make something of ourselves. These are misplaced desires.

- Sabbath rest opens the space for more creativity. It is an energy reset button God has given us.
- The image of God is better reflected than ingested.
- Creativity needs three things to grow: affirmation, focused work, and boundaries.
- Consistency yields credibility.

Chapter 6: Genius Gone Wrong

- When we live primarily out of our weaknesses, we will experience paralysis. When we live in our strengths, we will experience the thrill of creative stretching.
- Fear, pride, and comparison are silent genius assassins.
- Comparison leads to discouragement and individualism.
- Every human being is completely normal and completely unique at the same time.
- Celebrities, events, and start-ups have become idols in our culture.
- Love is essential to practicing redemptive creativity. Our creativity should yield worship to Him and love to the world around us.
- The key to ministry in the twenty-first century will be discovering, unlocking, and releasing people to live out their God-given abilities on a different stage.
- Christian leaders should function like doulas in the childbirth process. We can serve others by equipping, coaching, supporting, and comforting them as they live out the mission of God.

Chapter 7: The Church As Genius Factory

- Faith and obedience sit at the knife's edge of failure.
- We need to put our best energy into being saint equippers.
- Our focus on leadership development in the church should far exceed our focus on excellence.
- Most pastors in America are on a ministry treadmill, feeling exhausted but ineffective.
- The five typical responses to culture are to *condemn, critique, copy, consume,* and *create.* Take an honest assessment of how you and your ministry interact with culture.
- In Athens (Acts 17), Paul engages culture en route to creatively sharing the gospel. We should do the same.
- Churches should be genius labs. The family of God is the best space on the planet to develop leaders.
- We must learn to celebrate growth and development, not just the final product.
- Apprenticeships are crucial to spiritual and creative growth.
- Jesus was the most hospitable person who ever lived. He was always focused on outsiders and outcasts who lived on the fringes.

Chapter 8: Accidental Geniuses

- Pastors aren't at the center of God's vision for churches; God is.
- God gives us room to co-create with Him. He does the heavy lifting, but He invites us to join.

- Sometimes living within our genius feels as simple as plugging something in or flipping a switch. God wires the house; we plug in our gifts.
- Good creativity should be rooted in good theology.
- We need to affirm others for the unique genius they possess while reminding them of the path of humility.
- If people can find joy in doing something (play), they can find the desire to keep doing it (passion).
- We don't exist to be geniuses; we exist to be generous.
- Play + Passion + Purpose = a recipe to unleash God's people into impact.
- We have a creative and loving heavenly Father who created us in His image.
- Christ followers should become a sweet aroma to the world and spread the fame of Jesus.
- People are primarily seeking three things from churches today: convenience, consumption, and investment. Spend your best time with those who want to invest in God's mission.
- Don't use your gifts as weapons; use them as blessings.
- When pastors bless and affirm the work of a congregation outside of the walls it surprises and inspires people.

Chapter 9: Unleashing Geniuses

- Most opportunities don't look golden at first. God often chooses to birth beauty out of struggle.
- Plan B often turns into our greatest opportunity. Scarcity births clarity.

- Uncovering genius in others is not a call away from discipleship but a call to creatively reengage discipleship.
- Churches aren't about programs; they're about people. God loves people. He created people. We love people. People have great value.
- No one wants to be used, but everyone longs to be utilized.
- One of the best ways church leaders can guide artists is to connect them. The life of a creative can be lonely. Artists need to find other artists.
- Friendship yields trust. Partnership yields shared ownership. Collaboration yields cocreation.
- Forge friendship, develop partnerships, lean into collaboration, and watch the kingdom impact grow.
- Gospel unity can be a powerful apologetic. It can help those far from the church to see the heart of our God.
- Trust + Shared Ownership + Cocreation = Effective Team
- Six marks of a healthy team: partnership, learning, truth, celebration, listening, and storytelling.

Chapter 10: Go Ahead and Fail

- If your narrative doesn't allow for failure, your theology is brittle.
- Much of our genius is not tangible, but it is potential.
- Failure is unavoidable, especially in creative endeavors. Because we *have* a genius (instead of being the genius), we can neither receive all the praise or all the criticism.
- Taking your masterpiece from the basement to the gallery is one of the scariest things you can do.

- Here's the good news: You will fail. That's when grace and identity become real.
- Many of our views of successful, strong leadership are more cultural than biblical.
- Instead of *"Will it work?"* we must learn to ask, *"Should I try it?"*
- This is the time for a courageous church, not a fearful church.
- God never asks us to be successful; He asks us to be faithful. The gospel doesn't promise us surety; it invites us to risk.
- Where leaders create space for risk and failure, they will reap experimentation.
- Perhaps the greatest thing you can embed in a leadership culture is an obvious freedom to fail.
- Every act of obedience takes faith; some are just scarier than others.
- A risking church sends people out beyond its walls to impact communities. Just *doing* church isn't a risk, but *impacting* communities requires a culture of risk taking.
- Excellence matters, but faith matters more.
- Innovation only exists when failure is possible, even probable.

Chapter 11: How to Send a Genius Well

- Ministers of the gospel, paid or unpaid, must develop a creative imagination of how God might want to work in His people.

- Authenticity is a gift you offer and a practice you model.
- Four crucial actions to release genius in others: Remind others they have a genius. Observe and affirm their genius. Remind them their genius should be aimed at kingdom work. Get practical and help them find opportunities.
- God makes creative geniuses, but we affirm and launch them.
- A sending church invests in people, apprentices them for greatness, and lets go of them when it's time.
- What feels like a loss for a church is often a win for the kingdom.
- The metrics and aims of our church will determine much of our joy and emotions.
- It isn't unspiritual to measure things. Just make sure you're measuring the right things.
- When people observe leaders modeling what matters to a church and a community, they feel permission to join the party.
- Commissioning has always been a practice of God's people. It reminds us of three things: we see God's work in you, we are for you, and God is with you.
- Most churches don't give their leaders a kickoff, they punt them.
- Sending is an act of faith. It's not natural to develop leaders and willingly let go of your best.
- Commissioning is not a sign a leader is perfect or complete; it's a sign they are set apart and affirmed.

QUESTIONS FOR UNLEASHING GENIUS

This section can be used for unearthing your genius. This can be particularly helpful to share with a group.[1]

- What specific area is your sweet spot?
- What is worth doing even if you fail?
- What situations or seasons have borne the most fruit in your life?
- What are you better at than a thousand other people?
- What gifts has God uniquely given you?
- What areas of your job seem like pure joy instead of work?
- What needs do you love to meet in others?
- What environments do you love to be involved in? Why?
- What is your dream job? Why?
- What causes are you drawn to? (Refer to the list in the next section.)
- What dreams do you have for the church?
- What conversations do you like to be included in?
- What kinds of people do you naturally advocate for?
- What are your dreams for your community?

- What are your dreams for your family?
- What activities make you feel fully alive? Why?
- What things do you like to cultivate in others?
- What is your preferred medium of art?
- How do you dream of leveraging technology to help others?
- What do you continue to do when you aren't forced to?
- What does your ideal Sabbath day look like?
- What is your next step in the creative process?

POTENTIAL CAUSES
TO CHAMPION[1]

U se this section as a resource and idea factory for you and your team. Circle the causes you champion. Some of these are already in you, and you didn't even know it until you saw it on paper. Make sure to share them with others.

- Neighborhood connection
- Bullying/cyberbullying
- Art and culture creation
- Fair trade
- Nutrition
- City and neighborhood development
- Protection of public lands
- Engineering/built environment/city planning
- Racial tensions and reconciliation
- Environmental issues
- Empowerment of those on the fringes
- Men's and women's growth/biblical manhood and womanhood
- Mental illness
- HIV/AIDS

- Ethics
- Financial stewardship
- Job training
- Creation care
- Health and fitness
- Poverty and hunger
- Politics and policy
- Sexuality and gender issues
- Marriage
- Parenting
- Education and literacy
- Sanctity of human life/abortion alternatives
- Abuse/domestic violence
- Addiction: drugs, pornography, alcohol, technology, eating, sex, success
- Parenting
- Leadership development
- At-risk children
- Orphan care/adoption/foster care
- Career development and job creation
- Global issues
- Musical, poetic, and prophetic expression
- Technology expansion
- Entrepreneurship
- Women's empowerment
- Christian vocation
- Coffee
- Technology and innovation
- Increasing others' self-esteem
- Fighting sex trafficking
- Local transportation
- Other:

SOURCES

Allen, David. *Getting Things Done: The Art of Stress-Free Productivity*. Revised edition. New York: Penguin Books, 2015.

Berger, Jonah. *Contagious: Why Things Catch On*. New York: Simon & Schuster, 2013.

Catmull, Edwin E. *Creativity, Inc.: Overcoming the Unseen Forces That Stand in the Way of True Inspiration*. New York: Random House, 2014.

Catron, Jenni. *Clout: Discover and Unleash Your God-Given Influence*. Nashville: Thomas Nelson, 2014.

Chapman, Gary. *Sacred Pathways: Discover Your Soul's Path to God*. Grand Rapids, MI: Zondervan, 2010.

Crouch, Andy. *Culture Making: Recovering Our Creative Calling*. Downers Grove, IL: Intervarsity, 2008.

De Pree, Max. *Leadership Is an Art*. East Lansing: Michigan State University Press, 1987.

Dotzler, Ron. *Out of the Seats and into the Streets*. N.p.p.: CreateSpace, 2015.

Gardner, Howard E. *Intelligence Reframed*. New York: Basic Books, 2000.

Lewis, C. S. *The Joyful Christian: 127 Readings from C. S. Lewis*. New York: Macmillan, 1977.

McMahon, Darrin M. *Divine Fury: A History of Genius*. New York: Basic Books, 2013.

McManus, Erwin Raphael. *The Artisan Soul: Crafting Your Life into a Work of Art*. San Francisco: HarperOne, 2014.

McNeal, Reggie, *Missional Renaissance: Changing the Scorecard for the Church*. San Francisco: Jossey-Bass, 2009.

Palmer, Parker J. *Let Your Life Speak: Listening for the Voice of Vocation*. San Francisco: Jossey-Bass, 2000.

Rees, Erik. *S.H.A.P.E.: Finding and Fulfilling Your Unique Purpose for Life*. Grand Rapids, MI: Zondervan, 2006.

Robinson, Ken. *The Creative Epiphany*

Shenk, David. *The Genius in All of Us: Why Everything You've Been Told About Genetics, Talent, and IQ Is Wrong*. New York: Doubleday, 2010.

Smith, James K. A. *You Are What You Love: The Spiritual Power of Habit*. Grand Rapids, MI: Brazos Press, 2016.

Sprinkle, Preston M. *Go: Returning Discipleship to the Front Lines of Faith*. Colorado Springs: NavPress, 2016.

Stone, Douglas, and Sheila Heen. *Thanks for the Feedback: The Science and Art of Receiving Feedback Well (Even When It Is Off Base, Unfair, Poorly Delivered, and Frankly, You're Not in the Mood)*. New York: Viking, 2014.

Wagner, Tony. *Creating Innovators: The Making of Young People Who Will Change the World*. New York: Scribner, 2012.

Webber, Robert E., and Rodney Clapp. *People of the Truth: The Power of the Worshiping Community in the Modern World*. San Francisco: Harper & Row, 1988.

Wiseman, Liz. *Multipliers: How the Best Leaders Make Everyone Smarter*. New York: HarperBusiness, 2010.

HELPFUL RESOURCES ON UNLEASHING CREATIVITY

Berger, Jonah. *Contagious: Why Things Catch On*. New York: Simon & Schuster, 2013.

Catron, Jenni. *Clout: Discover and Unleash Your God-Given Influence*. Nashville: Thomas Nelson, 2014.

Crouch, Andy. *Culture Making: Recovering Our Creative Calling*. Downers Grove, IL: Intervarsity, 2008.

Duhigg, Charles. *The Power of Habit: Why We Do What We Do in Life and Business*. New York: Random House, 2012.

Gilbert, Elizabeth. *Big Magic*.

Gladwell, Malcolm. *The Tipping Point: How Little Things Can Make a Big Difference*. Boston: Little, Brown, 2000.

McKeown, Greg. *Essentialism: The Disciplined Pursuit of Less*. New York: Crown Business, 2014.

McManus, Erwin Raphael. *The Artisan Soul: Crafting Your Life into a Work of Art*. San Francisco: HarperOne, 2014.

Pressfield, Steven. *The War of Art: Break Through the Blocks and Win Your Inner Creative Battles*. New York: Warner Books, 2002.

Rees, Erik. *S.H.A.P.E.: Finding and Fulfilling Your Unique Purpose for Life*. Grand Rapids, MI: Zondervan, 2006.

Smith, James K. A. *You Are What You Love: The Spiritual Power of Habit*. Grand Rapids, MI: Brazos Press, 2016.

Stone, Douglas, and Sheila Heen. *Thanks for the Feedback: The Science and Art of Receiving Feedback Well (Even When It Is Off*

Base, Unfair, Poorly Delivered, and Frankly, You're Not in the Mood). New York: Viking, 2014.

Wiseman, Liz. *Multipliers: How the Best Leaders Make Everyone Smarter.* New York: HarperBusiness, 2010.

NOTES

Chapter 1: Where Does Genius Come From?

1. Darrin M. McMahon, *Divine Fury: A History of Genius* (New York: Basic Books, 2013), xiv.
2. McMahon, *Divine Fury*, xiv.
3. David Shenk, *The Genius in All of Us: Why Everything You've Been Told About Genetics, Talent, and IQ Is Wrong* (New York: Doubleday, 2010), 58.
4. Elizabeth Gilbert, "Your Elusive Creative Genius," *TED*, February 2009, https://www.ted.com/talks/elizabeth_gilbert_on_genius.
5. Max De Pree, *Leadership Is an Art* (East Lansing: Michigan State University Press, 1987), 3.
6. Robert E. Webber and Rodney Clapp, *People of the Truth: The Power of the Worshiping Community in the Modern World* (San Francisco: Harper & Row, 1988), 32.
7. Ibid., 33.
8. Ibid., 58.
9. Reggie McNeal, *Missional Renaissance: Changing the Scorecard for the Church* (San Francisco: Jossey-Bass, 2009), 170.
10. Andy Crouch, *Culture Making: Recovering Our Creative Calling* (Downers Grove, IL: InterVarsity, 2008), 40.

Chapter 2: What Counts?

1. J. R. Briggs and Bob Hyatt, *Mantras for Ministry: Language for Cultivating Kingdom Culture* (Grand Rapids: InterVarsity Press, 2016), 108.

2. Eugene Peterson, *The Pastor: A Memoir* (New York: HarperOne, 2012), 280.

3. Parker Palmer, *Let Your Life Speak: Listening for the Voice of Vocation* (New York: Jossey-Bass, 1999, 2012), 21.

4. Andy Crouch, *Culture Making: Recovering Our Creative Calling* (Downers Grove, IL: InterVarsity Press, 2013), 22.

5. Sir Ken Robinson, various *TED* talks, https://www.ted.com/talks.

6. Liz Wiseman and Greg McKeown, *Multipliers: How the Best Leaders Make Everyone Smarter* (New York: HarperBusiness, 2010), 26.

7. Alan Hirsch and Lance Ford, *Right Here, Right Now: Everyday Mission for Everyday People* (Ada, MI: Baker Books, 2011), 84.

8. Max DePree, *Leadership is an Art* (New York: Random House, 2004), 108.

9. Walter McKenzie, *Multiple Intelligences and Instructional Technology: Second Edition* (Danvers, MA: International Society for Technology in Education, 2005).

Chapter 3: Creative Espionage

1. Kevin Palau, *Unlikely: Setting Aside Our Differences to Live Out the Gospel* (New York: Howard Books, an imprint of Simon & Schuster, 2016), 159.

2. Preston Sprinkle, *Go: Returning Discipleship to the Front Lines of Faith* (Colorado Springs: NavPress, 2016), 78.

3. Ibid.

4. Ephesians 4:12 ESV.

5. 2013 Global Leadership Summit. http://www.willowcreek.com /events/leadership/vidhub.asp.

6. "Empower." Merriam-Webster.com. Accessed April 30, 2017. https://www.merriam-webster.com/dictionary/empower.

7. Andy Crouch, *Culture Making: Recovering Our Creative Calling* (Downers Grove, IL: InterVarsity, 2008), 43.

8. This comes from my friend Brian Mavis from the 2016 Neighboring Church gathering.

9. Daniel Im, *The Exchange* on Ed Stetzer's blog, April 9, 2015. http://www.christianitytoday.com/edstetzer/.

10. Liz Wiseman and Greg McKeown, *Multipliers: How the Best Leaders Make Everyone Smarter* (New York: HarperBusiness, 2010), 47.

11. Ibid., 48.

12. Ibid., 63.

13. Ibid., 61.

14. Jenni Catron, *Clout: Discover and Unleash Your God-Given Influence* (Nashville: Thomas Nelson, 2014), 25.

Chapter 4: The New Geniuses

1. Seth Godin, *Linchpin: Are You Indispensable?* (New York: Penguin Group, 2011), 8.

2. Andy Crouch, *Culture Making: Recovering Our Creative Calling* (Downers Grove, IL: InterVarsity, 2008), 67.

3. Similar thoughts from Erwin Raphael McManus in *Artisan Soul: Crafting Your Life into a Work of Art* (New York: HarperOne, 2015), 33.

4. Robert E. Webber and Rodney Clapp, *People of the Truth: The Power of the Worshiping Community in the Modern World* (San Francisco: Harper & Row, 1988), 90.

5. C. S. Lewis, *The Joyful Christian* (New York: Scribner, 1996), 137.

6. T. M. Amabile, "How to Kill Creativity," *Harvard Business Review* 76, no. 5 (September–October 1998): 76–87. http://www.hbs.edu/faculty/Pages/item.aspx?num=7420.

7. Seth Godin, *Linchpin: Are You Indispensable?* (New York: Penguin Group, 2011), 188.

8. Ibid., 83.

9. Preston Sprinkle, *Go: Returning Discipleship to the Front Lines of Faith* (Colorado Springs: NavPress, 2016), 98.

10. Ron Dotzler, *Out of the Seats and into the Streets* (CreateSpace Independent Publishing Platform, 2015), 65.

11. Ibid., 12.

Chapter 5: Genius Is a Process

1. David Shenk, *The Genius in All of Us: Why Everything You've Been Told About Genetics, Talent, and IQ Is Wrong* (New York: Doubleday, 2010).

2. Tony Wagner, *Creating Innovators: The Making of Young People Who Will Change the World* (New York: Scribner, 2015).

3. Darrin McMahon, *Divine Fury: A History of Genius* (New York: Perseus, 2013), xx intro.

4. David Shenk, *The Genius in All of Us: Why Everything You've Been Told About Genetics, Talent, and IQ Is Wrong* (New York: Doubleday, 2010), 122.

5. Elizabeth Gilbert, "Your Elusive Creative Genius," *TED*, February 2009, https://www.ted.com/talks/elizabeth_gilbert_on_genius.

6. John Maxwell from the 2016 Global Leadership Summit. https://tonymorganlive.com/2016/08/12/john-maxwell-global-leadership-summit-2016/.

7. David Shenk, *The Genius in All of Us: Why Everything You've Been Told About Genetics, Talent, and IQ Is Wrong* (New York: Doubleday, 2010), 66.

8. Ibid., 122.

9. Ibid., 71.

10. Ibid., 117

11. Andy Crouch, *Culture Making: Recovering Our Creative Calling* (Downers Grove, IL: InterVarsity, 2008), 22.

12. As discussed at length in Malcolm Gladwell's book *The Tipping Point: How Little Things Can Make a Big Difference* (New York: Bay Back, 2000, 2002).

13. I recommend Henry Cloud's book *Boundaries* or Warne Cordeiro's *Leading on Empty* for anyone getting started on this topic.

14. Parker J. Palmer, *Let Your Life Speak: Listening for the Voice of Vocation* (San Francisco: Jossey-Bass, 2000), 30.

15. Ibid., 41.

16. Kevin Palau, *Unlikely: Setting Aside Our Differences to Live Out the Gospel* (New York: Howard Books, an imprint of Simon & Schuster, 2016), 143.

Chapter 6: Genius Gone Wrong

1. Liz Wiseman and Greg McKeown, *Multipliers: How the Best Leaders Make Everyone Smarter* (New York: HarperBusiness, 2010), 62.
2. Rowan Williams, *The Sign and the Sacrifice: The Meaning of the Cross and Resurrection* (New York: Pilgrim, 1984), 83, as seen in Robert E. Webber and Rodney Clapp, *People of the Truth: The Power of the Worshiping Community in the Modern World* (San Francisco: Harper & Row, 1988), 61.
3. David Shenk, *The Genius in All of Us: Why Everything You've Been Told About Genetics, Talent, and IQ Is Wrong* (New York: Doubleday, 2010), 57.
4. Will Mancini and Max Lucado, *Church Unique: How Missional Leaders Cast Vision, Capture Culture, and Create Movement* (San Francisco: Jossey-Bass, 2008), 6.
5. James K. A. Smith, *You Are What You Love: The Spiritual Power of Habit* (Grand Rapids, MI: Baker Publishing Group, 2016), xii.
6. Henri Nouwen, *In the Name of Jesus: Reflections on Christian Leadership* (Chestnut Ridge, NY: Crossroad Publishing Company, 1989), 60.
7. Seth Godin, *Linchpin: Are You Indispensable?* (New York: Penguin Group, 2011), 7.
8. Erwin Raphael McManus in *Artisan Soul: Crafting Your Life into a Work of Art* (New York: HarperOne, 2015), 5.
9. "Doula." Merriam-Webster.com. Accessed April 30, 2017. https://www.merriam-webster.com/dictionary/doula.

Chapter 7: The Church as Genius Factory

1. Jenni Catron, *Clout: Discover and Unleash Your God-Given Influence* (Nashville: Thomas Nelson, 2014), 55.
2. Ed Catmull, *Creativity Inc.: Overcoming the Unseen Forces That Stand in the Way of True Inspiration* (New York: Random House, 2014), 108.
3. Tom Paterson, *Deeper, Richer, Fuller: Discover the Spiritual Life You Long For* (New York: Howard Books, a division of Simon & Schuster, 2010), 194.

4. Will Mancini and Max Lucado, *Church Unique: How Missional Leaders Cast Vision, Capture Culture, and Create Movement* (San Francisco: Jossey-Bass, 2008), 7.

5. Tony Wagner, *Creating Innovators: The Making of Young People Who Will Change the* World (New York: Scribner, 2015), 86.

6. Chase Jarvis, *The Best Camera Is the One That's with You: iPhone Photography* (Berkeley, CA: New Riders, 2010).

7. I give more on this paradigm shift in my book *Staying is the New Going: Choosing to Love Where God Places You* (Colorado Springs: NavPress, 2015).

8. Mark Batterson, *Chase the Lion: If Your Dream Doesn't Scare You, It's Too Small* (New York: Penguin Random House, 2016).

9. Andy Crouch, *Culture Making: Recovering Our Creative Calling* (Downers Grove, IL: InterVarsity, 2008), 68–70.

10. Ibid., 85.

11. James K. A. Smith talks about the search for "the good life" extensively in his book *You Are What You Love*: The Spiritual Power of Habit (Grand Rapids, MI: Baker Publishing Group, 2016).

12. Andy Crouch, *Culture Making: Recovering Our Creative Calling* (Downers Grove, IL: InterVarsity, 2008), 89.

13. Ibid., 73.

14. Probably from Epimenides of Crete.

15. From Aratus's Poem "Phainomena." http://www.theoi.com/Text/AratusPhaenomena.html.

16. I talk at length about apprenticeships in my book *Guardrails: Six Principles for Multiplying Church* (Colorado Springs: NavPress, 2016). The Venn diagram of relational, experiential, and formal learning has been life changing for me and has helped countless leaders understand how we strike a healthy balance for learning

17. Kevin Palau, *Unlikely: Setting Aside Our Differences to Live Out the Gospel* (New York: Howard Books, an imprint of Simon & Schuster, 2016), 137.

18. Howard Gardner, *Intelligence Reframed: Multiple Intelligences for the 21st Century* (New York: Basic Books, 1999), 126.

Chapter 8: Accidental Geniuses

1. Mother Teresa, *No Greater Love* (Novato, CA: New World Library, 2001), 55.
2. Erwin Raphael McManus in *Artisan Soul: Crafting Your Life into a Work of Art* (New York: HarperOne, 2015), 5.
3. I talk more about this in depth in my book *Guardrails: Six Principles for Multiplying Church* (Colorado Springs: NavPress, 2016), as the fourth step of submission to God in ministry.
4. Andy Crouch, *Culture Making: Recovering Our Creative Calling* (Downers Grove, IL: InterVarsity, 2008), 110.
5. Will Mancini and Max Lucado, *Church Unique: How Missional Leaders Cast Vision, Capture Culture, and Create Movement* (San Francisco: Jossey-Bass, 2008), 8–9.
6. Great thoughts from my friend Mike Worley Jr. of Clymb Marketing. http://www.clymbmarketing.com/.
7. Nouwen talks about this and shares his story of practicing this throughout his book *In the Name of Jesus*: Reflections on Christian Leadership (Chestnut Ridge, NY: Crossroad Publishing Company, 1989). It's a must-read!
8. Tony Wagner, *Creating Innovators: The Making of Young People Who Will Change the World* (New York: Scribner, 2015), 26
9. Seth Godin, *Linchpin: Are You Indispensable?* (New York: Penguin Group, 2011), 229.
10. Erwin Raphael McManus, *The Artisan Soul: Crafting Your Life into a Work of Art* (New York: HarperOne, 2014), 9.
11. I am referencing Ying Kai's story in *T4T*. I talk at length about how 20–25 percent of spiritual leaders tend to be reproducers in my book *Guardrails: Six Principles for a Multiplying Church* (Colorado Springs: NavPress, 2016).
12. Kevin Palau, *Unlikely: Setting Aside Our Differences to Live Out the Gospel* (New York: Howard Books, an imprint of Simon & Schuster, 2016), 148.

Chapter 9: Unleashing Geniuses

1. Ed Catmull, *Creativity Inc.: Overcoming the Unseen Forces That Stand in the Way of True Inspiration* (New York: Random House, 2014), 131.

2. Kevin Palau, *Unlikely: Setting Aside Our Differences to Live Out the Gospel* (New York: Howard Books, an imprint of Simon & Schuster, 2016), 149.

3. Jonah Berger, *Contagious: Why Things Catch On* (New York: Simon & Schuster, 2013), 24.

4. He tells this story at DaveRamsey.com.

5. I recommend Alan Hirsch's classic *The Forgotten Ways* as a beautiful look at recovering ancient principles for modern impact.

6. Ed Catmull, *Creativity Inc.: Overcoming the Unseen Forces That Stand in the Way of True Inspiration* (New York: Random House, 2014), 75.

7. Henri Nouwen, *In the Name of Jesus: Reflections on Christian Leadership* (Chestnut Ridge, NY: Crossroad Publishing Company, 1989), 18–19.

8. David Kinnaman, *You Lost Me: Why Young Christians Are Leaving Church . . . and Rethinking Faith* (Grand Rapids, MI: Baker Publishing Group, 2011), 101.

9. James K. A. Smith, *You Are What You Love: The Spiritual Power of Habit* (Grand Rapids, MI: Baker Publishing Group, 2016), 180.

10. A great source for any artist is the book by Makoto Fujimura, *Refractions: A Journey of Faith, Art, and Culture* (Colorado Springs: NavPress, 2009).

11. Douglas Stone and Sheila Heen, *Thanks for the Feedback: The Science and Art of Receiving Feedback Well* (New York: Penguin, 2014), 20.

12. Cooper, *Getting Things Done*, 64.

13. Parker Palmer, *Let Your Life Speak: Listening for the Voice of Vocation* (New York: Jossey-Bass, 1999, 2012), 4.

14. Jonah Berger, *Contagious: Why Things Catch On* (New York: Simon & Schuster, 2013), 181.

15. I borrowed this idea from my friend Kevin Goos.
16. Tony Wagner, *Creating Innovators: The Making of Young People Who Will Change the World* (New York: Scribner, 2015), 12.
17. See Ephesians 4:11–12.

Chapter 10: Go Ahead and Fail

1. Erwin Raphael McManus, *The Artisan Soul: Crafting Your Life into a Work of Art* (New York: HarperOne, 2014), 43.
2. Douglas Stone and Sheila Heen, *Thanks for the Feedback: The Science and Art of Receiving Feedback Well* (New York: Penguin, 2014), 23.
3. James K. A. Smith, *You Are What You Love: The Spiritual Power of Habit* (Grand Rapids, MI: Baker Publishing Group, 2016), 107.
4. Howard Gardner, *Intelligence Reframed: Multiple Intelligences for the 21st Century* (New York: Basic Books, 1999), 34.
5. Erwin Raphael McManus, *The Artisan Soul: Crafting Your Life into a Work of Art* (New York: HarperOne, 2014), 35.
6. Throughout the book by Brene Brown, *Daring Greatly: How the Courage to Be Vulnerable Transforms the Way We Live, Love, Parent, and Lead* (New York: Avery, 2015).
7. Ed Catmull, *Creativity Inc.: Overcoming the Unseen Forces That Stand in the Way of True Inspiration* (New York: Random House, 2014), 108.
8. Phrase is repeated throughout the book by Helen Oxenbury and Michael Rosen, *We're going on a Bear Hunt* (New York: Simon & Schuster, 1989).

Chapter 11: How to Send a Genius Well

1. To hear the Truefaced Story, head to trueface.org.
2. This was coined by Malcolm Gladwell and explained in his book *The Tipping Point: How Little Things Can Make a Big Difference* (New York: Bay Back, 2000, 2002).
3. I borrowed this, okay I stole it, from my friend Scott Bloyer. I used this phrase weekly, maybe more.

4. Liz Wiseman and Greg McKeown, *Multipliers: How the Best Leaders Make Everyone Smarter* (New York: HarperBusiness, 2010), 215.

5. Reggie McNeal, *Missional Renaissance: Changing the Scorecard for the Church* (San Francisco: Jossey-Bass, 2009),160.

6. This was written by my friend Richie Fike. He is a talented musician and wordsmith.

Epilogue

1. Revelation 2:7, 11, 17, 29; 3:6, 13, 22.

Questions for Unleashing Genius

1. Modified from Erik Rees, *S.H.A.P.E.: Finding and Fulfilling Your Unique Purpose for Life* (Grand Rapids, MI: Zondervan, 2006).

Potential Causes to Champion

1. Help from Erik Rees, *S.H.A.P.E.: Finding and Fulfilling Your Unique Purpose for Life* (Grand Rapids, MI: Zondervan, 2006).

ABOUT THE AUTHOR

Alan Briggs is the director of Frontline Church Planting, a network and equipping hub in Colorado. He is the Multiplying Pastor at Vanguard Church in Colorado Springs where he makes disciples and trains leaders to multiply. He is also the lead creative at Stay Forth Designs, a leadership development team that equips leaders for health and impact through speaking, coaching, and consulting. His speaking and writing focus on equipping and unlocking the saints for effective ministry inside and outside the family of God. His previous books *Staying is the New Going* (2015) and *Guardrails* (2016), call followers of Jesus to both faithfulness and fruitfulness.

Alan and his wife, Julie, have four kids, two adopted and two biological, and are enjoying the process of growing roots. Their family focuses on building bridges to the lost, largely in the context of their neighborhood. He is passionate about equipping leaders and churches to multiply through relational, experiential, and formal learning. He loves climbing, camping, grilling, and connecting with his neighbors.

@AlanBriggs AlanBriggs.net

STAY FORTH DESIGNS

EQUIPPING LEADERS FOR HEALTH AND KINGDOM IMPACT

Part of my ministry is helping leaders and organizations get healthy and thrive. Stay Forth coaching and consulting helps leaders and organizations live into God's unique design for them. Every leader needs to learn processes that can enable them to dig in and bear lasting fruit. Stay Forth offers various venues for growing as a leader or a team.

For more information and booking, visit

StayForth.com

ALSO FROM ALAN BRIGGS

Staying is the New Going   Guardrails

Visit AlanBriggs.net for more information.

ALSO AVAILABLE FROM

NEXT

LEADERSHIP NETWORK

WHEREVER BOOKS ARE SOLD

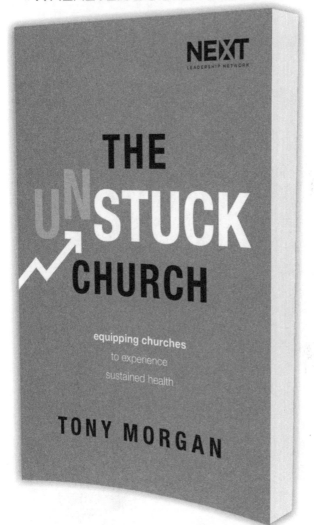

ISBN: 9780718094416
ISBN: 9780718094478 (E-BOOK)

ALSO AVAILABLE FROM

NEXT
LEADERSHIP NETWORK

WHEREVER BOOKS ARE SOLD

ISBN: 9780718096465
ISBN: 9780718096489 (E-BOOK)